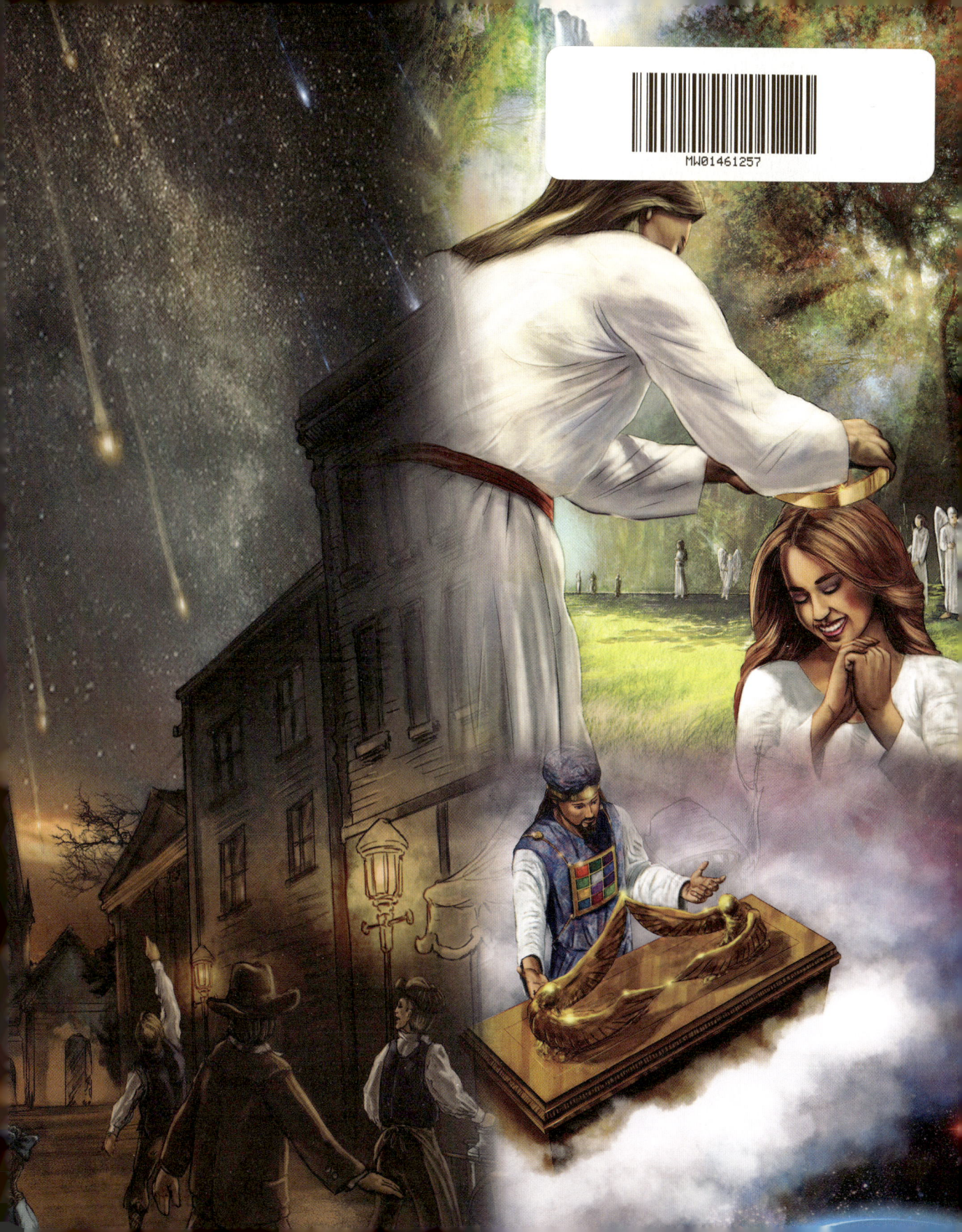

ISBN 978-1-629131-09-2

Copyright © 2017 by Remnant Publications, Inc.
Images Copyright © 2017 by Remnant Publications, Inc.
All Rights Reserved

Published by
Remnant Publications, Inc.
649 East Chicago Road
Coldwater, MI 49036

Scripture taken from the New King James Version®. Copyright © 1982 by Thomas Nelson. Used by permission. All rights reserved.

0919

Text written by Bradley Booth
Copyedited by Rudy Hall, Judy Jennings, Clarissa Fiedler
Edited by Lori Peckham, Jerry Stevens
Cover design by David Berthiaume
Interior design by Eric Pletcher
Cover illustrations by Leandro Tonelli

Portions taken from the original works of E. G. White: *Patriarchs and Prophets, Prophets and Kings, The Desire of Ages, The Acts of the Apostles,* and *The Great Controversy.*

Printed in China

Note: This volume includes the stories of many individuals who God has used in a special way in history until our time. These stories are well documented in standard history works. They are told here to serve as an inspiration to today's families and to show God's prophetic working until He comes again.

Children's Century Classics

The Greatest Battle

Table of Contents

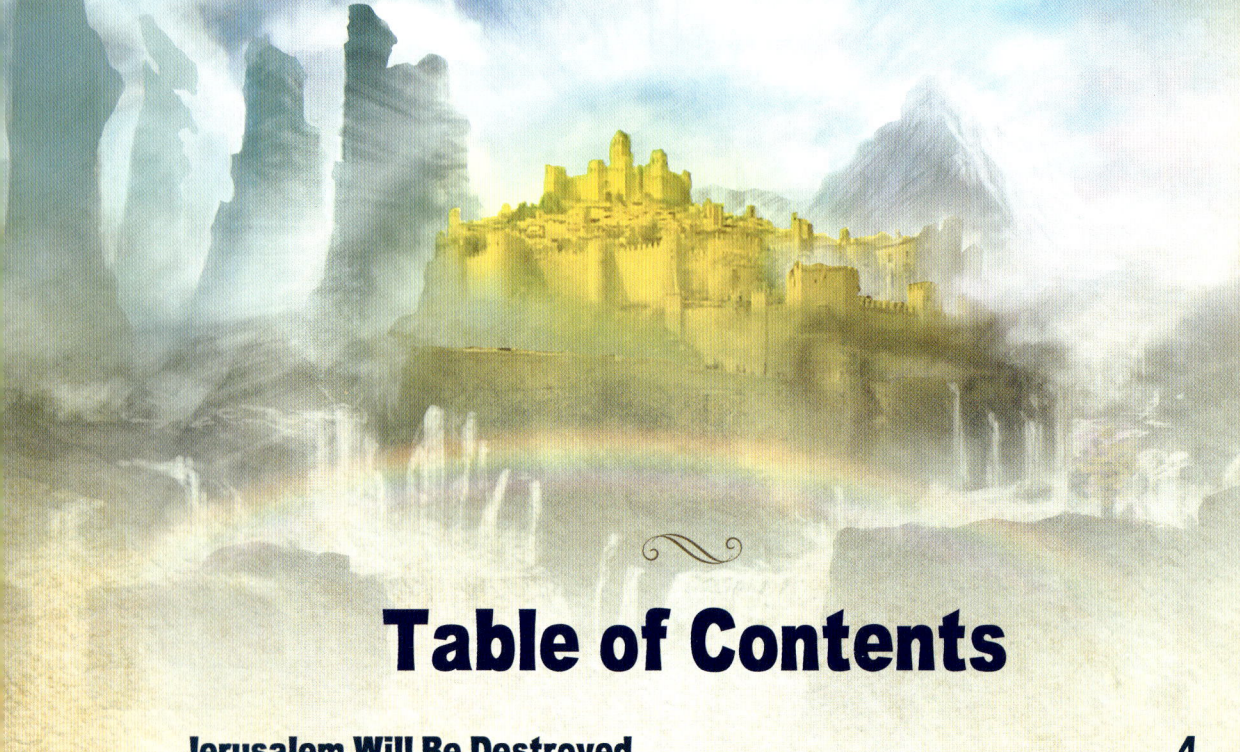

Jerusalem Will Be Destroyed 4
Satan Tries to Stamp Out the Christian Church 10
Church of the Dark Ages 16
The Waldenses 22
John Wycliffe 28
Huss and Jerome 32
Martin Luther as a Young Man 36
Martin and the Scary Staircase 40
Martin Luther Goes to Court 44
Revival in Switzerland 48
The French Reformation 52
Bow or Burn at the Stake 58
Tyndale the Translator 62
John Bunyan Jailed 68

Christians Flee to America	72
Roger Williams	76
Saved From a Fire	80
Two Brothers Dedicated to God	84
God Is Banned in France	88
Bloody Moon and Falling Stars	92
A Little Boy Makes a Big Decision	98
William Miller	102
God Chooses a Simple Farmer	106
Great Disappointment	110
God Gives a Long Look Into the Future	114
God's Special Day	118
What's Going On in the Courts of Heaven?	122
The Greatest Battle	126
Satan's Deadly Tricks	132
What Happens When We Die?	136
A Storm Is Coming	140
The Amazing Word of God	146
The Final Warning	152
Time of Trouble for God's People	158
Jesus to the Rescue	164
Locked up for 1,000 Years	168
God's Perfect Playground	174
Title Index: Complete List of Stories	178
Topical Index	183
Men and Women of the Bible	186

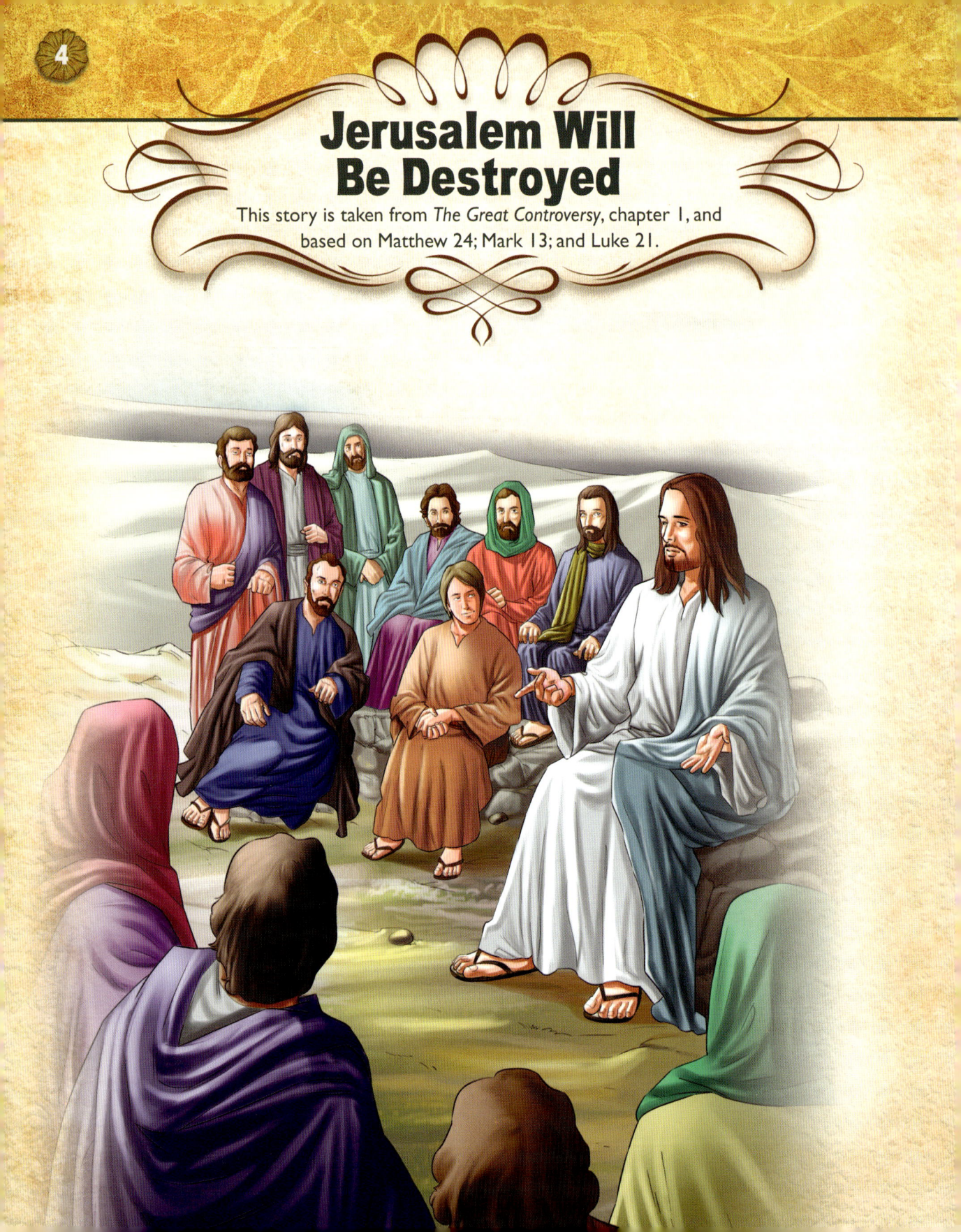

Jerusalem Will Be Destroyed

This story is taken from *The Great Controversy*, chapter 1, and based on Matthew 24; Mark 13; and Luke 21.

Jerusalem was an astounding city. It was called the City of David and Mount Zion in its earliest days after David made it the capital of Israel.

In Jesus' day, it stood proud and tall. Everybody thought that this great city would last forever. However, there would come a day when the beloved city would fall. Just before His death, Jesus predicted the destruction of Jerusalem and the magnificent temple. "Do you see all these things?" He said to His disciples as they looked at the massive stones set in the walls. "There is coming a day when not one of these stones will be left standing. Everything will be thrown down."

The disciples were shocked and could hardly believe their ears. Was Jesus telling them the truth? Was this possible? Jerusalem and the temple walls were built with gigantic stones. In fact, one stone was as big as a bus! It weighed almost one million pounds. Building the walls had taken years of incredible effort, and tearing them down would be just as difficult.

In Jesus' day, Jerusalem stood proud and tall. Everybody thought that this great city would last forever.

"How and when will this terrible event happen?" the disciples asked. "And what will be the signs that the time is near?"

"When you see the armies of the enemy surround Jerusalem, then you will know that it is almost time," Jesus replied. That would be the time for everyone to plan their escape. "Those who are working in their gardens or on their rooftops are not to spend time packing," He said. They wondered, "How will the Christians escape if they are surrounded?"

But the Jews refused to believe the words of Jesus. "God would never let Jerusalem be destroyed," they said. "Isn't Jerusalem God's Holy City? Didn't He promise that the temple would stand forever?" Jesus' talking only made the Jews angry. They were so proud and always bragging about what a great temple they had. The religious leaders loved the temple and hated Jesus. Instead of listening to Jesus so that they could be ready to escape when they had a chance, they got so angry at what He was saying that they wanted to kill Him. Here was their chance not only to escape from a terrible army that would be coming in the future; Jesus could also save them right now from their sins if they would just listen.

The final days of mercy ended for the Jews less than 40 years after Jesus went back to heaven. Everything happened just as He had said it would.

The Jews fought against Roman rule in A.D. 66, and that brought the Roman armies down into Judea to put down the revolution. The Roman general Cestius surrounded the city of Jerusalem and began a siege. The Roman army would not let anyone or anything into the city, which meant that no food or supplies were coming into the city.

The Roman general Cestius surrounded the city of Jerusalem and began a siege.

The Christians who were still in Jerusalem at the time were very worried. Jesus had said that they must try to escape, but how could they? They were surrounded by the Roman army!

The Jewish leaders in Jerusalem were worried too. They realized that they didn't have any hope of surviving a Roman siege. The Romans almost never gave up until they conquered their enemies.

The revolutionaries in Jerusalem were about ready to surrender when suddenly, without warning, General Cestius withdrew his armies from Jerusalem and began marching them back to the coast. This gave the Jewish revolutionaries courage, and they decided to chase the Roman army back to the coast. They attacked them at a place called Beth Horon, and, to everyone's surprise, they won. The Roman army suffered a terrible defeat, and the Jewish fighters returned to Jerusalem in triumph.

Meanwhile, back in Jerusalem, the Christians realized that they were free to leave. Now they could escape as Jesus had told them to. The Roman army and the revolutionaries had left the city, so there was no one to stop them. Quickly they left, taking with them only what they could carry. They fled as fast as they could to the city of Pella east of the Jordan.

Their victory against the Roman army made the revolutionaries even bolder than they had been before. "God has preserved us and the Holy City of Jerusalem," they said. "And He will continue to protect us."

Of course, this wasn't true. God was just giving them the chance to escape. The Jews had rejected Jesus as the Messiah and the Savior of the world. They had persecuted the Christians without mercy, killing many of them. They had rejected God, and He was now rejecting them. They were no longer His people.

For seven years before the final destruction of Jerusalem, a mysterious prophet had walked up and down its streets warning everyone that Jerusalem was about to be destroyed. No one listened, and the Jewish leaders finally locked him up in prison to keep him quiet.

In A.D. 70, when the Roman general Titus surrounded the city for the final time, the Jewish people still believed that their city could not be conquered. It was the week of the Passover, so there were millions of people in the city.

But Jerusalem's day of doom had finally come. Within three weeks General Titus had broken through two of the outer city walls.

The siege continued for seven months because the temple walls were too strong for them to break through. By then, the rebel groups in the city were battling against one another for territory and food. In the fighting that followed, fires broke out, which destroyed the city's supply of food. With millions of people in the city, disease and starvation now made conditions even worse.

No one trusted anyone. Friends would steal from friends, and children would snatch the food out of the mouths of their elderly parents. People were so hungry that they tried to eat their leather belts and sandals. Thousands died from starvation!

When people tried to sneak out at night to hunt for wild plants, they were caught, and if they resisted, they were crucified. Hundreds were put to death every day. At one point, the hills surrounding Jerusalem were so crowded with crosses that Roman soldiers could hardly walk among them.

During a skirmish one night between Roman soldiers and the Jewish revolutionaries, fires got out of control.

General Titus knew that the beautiful Jewish temple was one of the wonders of the Roman world. As the city was being destroyed, he commanded that the temple should not be touched. However, just as Jesus had predicted, the temple was demolished. The Roman soldiers were so angry at the horrors of starvation and murder that they saw in the city that they just wanted to end it all. During a skirmish one night between Roman soldiers and the Jewish revolutionaries, fires got out of control. A Roman soldier jammed a torch between the hinges of a door to the inner sanctuary, and the whole place caught on fire.

And so it was that Jerusalem was destroyed, just as Jesus had predicted. The city of the great king was no more. If the Jews had believed Jesus' words, they might have prevented this day of judgment. If they had accepted Jesus as their Savior, they would have remained His chosen people.

Our Prayer:

"Dear Father in heaven, forgive us when we don't listen to Your words of warning."

Hidden Treasure Questions:

✓ What were the names of the two Roman generals who attacked Jerusalem?

✓ How many people were in Jerusalem when the Romans surrounded it?

Listen to this story online!

Scan for bonus content

Satan Tries to Stamp Out the Christian Church

This story is taken from *The Great Controversy*, chapter 2, and based on Matthew 24; Luke 19; John 15; Acts 4-8; and Revelation 2.

Following the death of Jesus, His followers boldly preached the message of His death, resurrection, and Second Coming. Most were not educated and few had money, but they became powerful missionaries for their Savior. The power of the Holy Spirit went with them at every step, and soon the gospel of Jesus was the most popular news in Palestine. The message brought hope and courage to the hearts of people everywhere who had heard the story of salvation. Thousands were converted in a day.

However, Satan was not willing to give up without a fight, and he now inspired wicked people to persecute the young church! Stephen was the first to die as a martyr in Jerusalem for preaching the gospel. The Christians in Jerusalem were discouraged when Stephen died because he was one of their greatest champions. But, of course, they remembered Jesus' words when He said, "You will be brought before governors and kings for My sake, as a testimony to them and to the Gentiles" (Matthew 10:18).

He had also said: "Blessed are those who are persecuted for righteousness' sake, for theirs is the kingdom of heaven…. Rejoice and be exceedingly glad, for great is your reward in heaven, for so they persecuted the prophets who were before you" (Matthew 5:10-12).

"If they have persecuted Me, they will also persecute you," Jesus had said. Then He had shared that "this gospel of the kingdom will be preached in all the world" (Matthew 24:14).

Then James the brother of John was killed by Herod. Whenever the disciples preached in Jerusalem they were in danger of being arrested, beaten, or killed. So instead of staying together in one place, they scattered in every direction. All the apostles eventually left to serve God in the countries surrounding Judea and far beyond. Early Christian writers tell us that some of the disciples even went to Britain, Africa, and as far away as India. But no matter what the price, their greatest joy was to testify of their love for Jesus.

And like Stephen and James, many died for Jesus.

> **Stephen was the first to die as a martyr in Jerusalem for preaching the gospel.**

Both Peter and Paul died as martyrs under the great persecutions against Christians by the Roman emperor Nero. Every time a disciple of Christ was killed, others would take their place. Satan was losing this battle because the church was growing in spite of the persecution.

In the 40 years following the death of Jesus, the Christians preached the gospel to every known place on earth. By the time Paul died, it is estimated that there were a million Christians in the Roman Empire.

But though the gospel story was a popular one, Christians continued to be persecuted for their faith. They were driven from their homes to live in the wilderness and caves of the mountains. Others were caught and tortured, but they would not give up their faith. They knew Jesus had promised that even if they were killed, if they were faithful, God would raise them up and take them to be with Him in heaven. Still others had trials, mockings, scourgings, chains, and imprisonment.

As the number of Christians grew, so did the brutal persecutions. Thousands were imprisoned and slain, but others sprang up to fill their places. Domitian, who ruled Rome near the turn of the century, was especially cruel,

> **They were driven from their homes to live in the wilderness and caves of the mountains. Others were caught and tortured.**

executing Christians without mercy! They tried to kill the disciple John by boiling him in a pot of oil, but he was saved by a miracle from God. When he couldn't be killed, they finally took him to an island where they kept prisoners. This island was called Patmos. This didn't stop John, because it was on this island that he wrote the book of Revelation.

However, it was probably the Roman emperor Diocletian who had the worst record for persecuting Christians. During his time, torturing and executing followers of Jesus became a popular form of entertainment. In the Roman sports amphitheaters they were crucified, burned as torches, and fed to wild beasts. Clearly, it was Satan's wish to stamp out the Christian church. But through it all, the Christians maintained their faith in God's promises of eternal life.

The terrible persecutions that Satan hoped would break the church failed. The more bad things he did to the Christians, the more faithful was their loyalty to the gospel command given by Jesus Himself when He said, "Go therefore and make disciples of all the nations, baptizing them in the name of the Father and of the Son and of the Holy Spirit" (Matthew 28:19).

Satan finally realized that no matter what he did to hurt the church, it was still growing. So he decided to change his strategy. Since the Christians would not give up their faith by force, Satan decided he would use deceit. Persecution stopped, and Satan tried to convince the Christians that it was OK to do whatever they wanted. God would still approve of them. Unfortunately, many were tricked into believing this lie.

By the time the Roman emperor Constantine came into power, there were so many Christians that he decided to use them to unite his empire. To many Christians this looked like a wonderful thing, but those who were studying the Scriptures could see the dangers. Rome was still a pagan empire. Everyone in the Roman Empire worshipped all kinds of false gods. So Emperor Constantine said, "Let's make a law that we all worship on the same day." By doing this, he believed that everybody could get along together. But that definitely wasn't God's plan.

Sure enough, under Constantine the Sabbath began to be changed from Saturday to Sunday. And following this, other false teachings crept into the church too, such as the worshipping of saints and the idea of an eternally burning hell.

Fortunately, there were many Christians who decided they did not want to be a part of those falsehoods. Thankfully, they separated themselves to keep the church pure.

The Christian church has been persecuted for following Jesus down through the ages. We sometimes wonder, "Why would God allow His church to be persecuted?" But we must remember that Jesus suffered at the hands of Satan when He was on earth too. This shows us who Satan really is. He is the greatest enemy of God, and that makes him our enemy too.

Under Constantine the Sabbath began to be changed from Saturday to Sunday.

He wants people to think that God is mean and cruel because He doesn't keep Christians from dying during these terrible times of persecution. But the truth cannot be denied. Satan is the one who is mean and cruel! He is the one who has hunted down the Christians to kill them! And sadly, he saved his worst treatment for the Son of God when he crucified Him on a cross.

We may not always understand why there has to be suffering in this world. However, it is because of the death of Jesus that you and I receive salvation today. Bad things do happen to God's people sometimes, but Jesus promises us that if we are faithful until death, He will give us a crown of life.

And so even if Satan hates God's church in the world today, we know that God will help us to be faithful to Him.

Our Prayer:

"Dear Father in heaven, I pray I will be as faithful to You as the Christian martyrs were down through the ages."

Hidden Treasure Questions:

✓ Who were some of the worst persecutors of Christians among the Roman emperors?

✓ What was the name of the first Roman emperor to become a Christian?

Listen to this story online!

Scan for bonus content

Church of the Dark Ages

This story is taken from *The Great Controversy*, chapter 3, and based on Genesis 2; Daniel 7; Luke 4; 2 Thessalonians 2; and Revelation 2.

During the centuries since the time of Jesus, the Christian church has changed so much. In the beginning, the church was pure, humble, and willing to go anywhere and make any sacrifice for Jesus and the gospel. Satan had persecuted the church relentlessly, but it had remained faithful and grown in spite of the worst he could throw at it.

However, as time passed, Satan realized that peace and prosperity might be better weapons against the church than persecution. If he wanted the church to fall, he was going to have to get it to give up its faith. This could be done only if he could get the church to stop doing some of the things Jesus and the Bible had taught them to do.

So the mystery of iniquity began in the church, as warned by Paul (2 Thessalonians 2:3-7). Slowly Satan began to introduce false teachings into the church. It began with Constantine, who became a Christian because it was the popular thing to do. As emperor, he helped bring more people into the church by making Sunday a Christian and pagan holiday in one. This secular holiday would eventually take the place of the seventh-day Sabbath in the church.

Other emperors who followed Constantine helped add other false teachings. Some of these included worshipping angels and dead saints, praying to Mary instead of to Jesus, believing in purgatory as a temporary state of punishment, and hell as a place where people suffer endlessly, and worshipping images and crosses.

The world now entered the time that we often call the "Dark Ages," and the church went with it. The Dark Ages era was a terrible time for everybody. It was a time of castles, moats, and Knights of the Round Table. It was a time of poverty, when people were so poor that they could be bought and sold with the land that they farmed.

Slowly false teachings were introduced into the church. It began with Constantine, who became a Christian because it was the popular thing to do.

The Dark Ages period in history was when there were no schools for common people, so knowledge came almost to a standstill. Few could read or write, so that meant no one could read the Bible for themselves. They had to depend on church leaders to read it for them. And to make matters worse, the only copies of the Bible available were written in Latin, a dead language that they didn't speak anymore.

As a result of no one reading or going to school, the lives of the people changed in other ways as well. They didn't know how to stay healthy. People got sick from diseases because they didn't know about germs. They didn't know which foods would keep them healthy or even that washing their hands before they ate could save their lives. Because of all these health issues, many people died. At that time, the average person in Europe lived to be only about 30 years of age.

Ignorance and superstition were so deep that it seemed the whole world had fallen asleep spiritually.

The Dark Ages also became a period of great superstition. Satan knew that if he could get people to be afraid, he could get them to believe anything. During those times, people believed less and less in the power of God, and more and more in the power of ghosts, goblins, witches, and werewolves.

It was during those times that the church began to paint a picture of Satan that became quite popular, though completely wrong. Instead of being an angel of light as the Bible teaches, church leaders said that he was an ugly creature with horns and a tail.

The Dark Ages became a time of great spiritual darkness because of all this. The ignorance and superstition were so deep that it seemed the whole world had fallen asleep spiritually. This meant that the church leaders could tell people whatever they wanted, and no one would know what was right or wrong. No one would challenge them because they were too afraid. If someone disagreed with something that the church was teaching, the leaders could excommunicate them and put them out of the church. Then they could send them to burn forever in hell when they died. Of course, this wasn't true. The Bible didn't teach any of these things, but no one knew any better because they could not read the Bible.

The bishop of Rome, also called the pope in those days, ruled like an emperor from Rome. As a church leader, he claimed that he was always right and could never be wrong spiritually. The word most often used for him was "infallible," which meant that he could not be wrong.

Of course, we all know that it wasn't true. The pope is just a man, and that makes him a sinner. The Son of God is the only One on earth who has never sinned.

But that didn't stop the pope from taking all the power that he could get. And as the years passed, the popes grew in power, and the church became fabulously wealthy. Soon the popes had gained power over every country in Europe and were telling kings and queens what they could and could not do. Kings could not be crowned without permission from the church, which now had absolute power. If a country didn't like it, the pope could send in an army to enforce the law.

And if the rulers of countries still didn't obey the pope, he could excommunicate them from the church. This was something leaders in Europe feared more than anything, and it usually made them think twice about questioning him.

Of course, this was all against the truths found in the Bible, but because everyone was ignorant about what the Bible taught, no one knew better.

One story from medieval times tells about a German emperor named Henry IV. He decided that he wasn't going to obey the pope for some reason, and was promptly excommunicated from the church. He was also forced to step down from his throne. The emperor was afraid that his royal princes might desert him, but what could he do? He wished he had obeyed the pope, but it was a little late for that now.

Pope Gregory VII made the emperor wait in an outdoor courtyard for three days, barefoot in the snow.

If he wanted his throne back, somehow he was going to have to make peace with the pope in Rome. But it wouldn't be easy. To do this, he would have to travel across the mountains in the middle of the winter to the castle where Pope Gregory VII was staying.

But the pope wouldn't see him. He made him wait in an outdoor courtyard for three days, barefoot in the snow and without a hat. Finally, the pope agreed to see him and accepted his apology, but by now the emperor had been greatly humbled. When word of the story got out, kings and princes in Europe were even more afraid of the pope and other leaders of the church.

And so it was that the control of the church tightened its grip on the governments of Europe. As the ignorance and superstition deepened, so did the times of spiritual darkness.

Our Prayer:

"Dear God, I pray that You will open the eyes of many in churches today where they do not teach the truths of the Bible."

Hidden Treasure Questions:

✓ What is the name for the period in history this chapter is talking about?

✓ What are some of the false teachings that have crept into the Christian church?

Listen to this story online!

Scan for bonus content

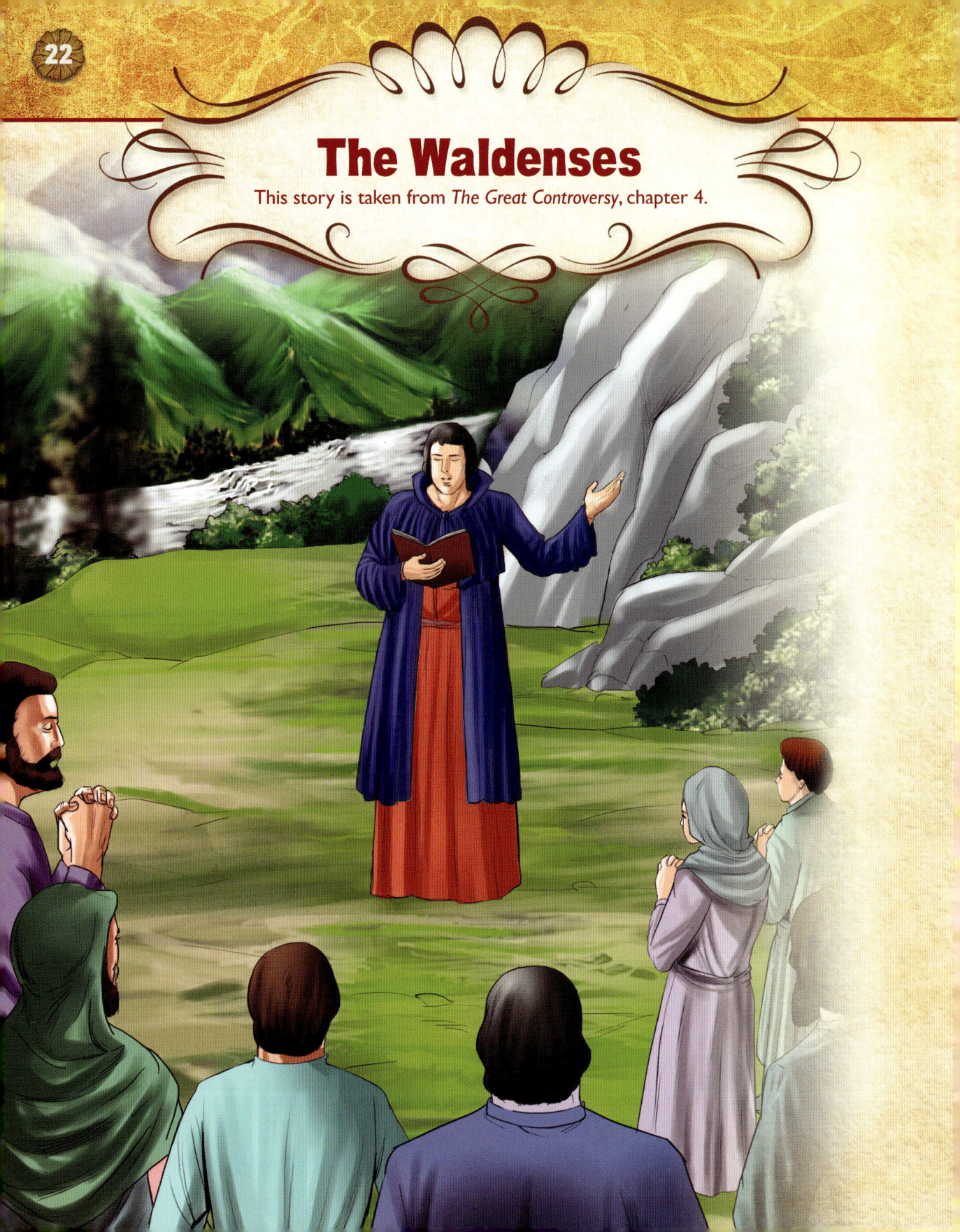

The Waldenses

This story is taken from *The Great Controversy*, chapter 4.

The story of the Waldenses is one of the saddest and yet most remarkable stories in all of history. It is about a group of people who were willing to be true to Jesus through good times and bad, to put the Bible first in their lives, and in many cases to die for their faith.

> **They were a godly people and wished to use the Bible as their only rule of faith.**

Nearly 1,000 years ago a religious group of Christians lived in Lyon, France. They were a godly people and wished to use the Bible as their only rule of faith. The Roman Church was very powerful in those days and did not want the Waldenses to ignore the traditional teachings of the church. Led by Peter Waldo, the Waldenses refused to obey the church and were soon being persecuted for their desire to follow the Bible and the Bible only.

The Waldenses eventually moved into the high country of the Swiss Alps because of this persecution. For many years, they lived in the mountain valleys hidden away from the world. They raised cattle and sheep and planted grain to harvest so that they could provide food for their families. They taught their children how to read and write. They told their children how important it was to make copies of the Bible to share with others. They required them to memorize long passages of Scripture in case their Bibles were ever taken away from them.

However, the quiet, peace-loving Waldenses were not satisfied working their farms and raising their families. They remembered that Jesus had asked His followers to become missionaries so that they could spread the gospel story to those who did not know the wonderful truths of the Bible.

So the men would take trips into the lowlands to the cities of the coastland and plain. There they would go as merchants or peddlers and sell things that they knew people might want. Some Waldensian travelers would sell jewels. Some would trade silks or other fine cloth. But they always carried with them hidden copies of passages from the Bible in case they should meet someone who might want to hear its precious truths. Many times they would sew these passages into their coats to avoid detection.

Satan was not happy with the Waldensian missionaries. They were a group of people who were not deceived by the false teachings of the church. They read their Bibles for themselves and taught others to follow their example. Hearts were changed, and many were led to Christ for the first time. So Satan, the enemy of God, planned and plotted as to how he could destroy them completely.

Through the church, Satan began a time of terrible persecution such as had never been seen before. A decree went out from the powerful church leader calling on all members of the church to wipe out the Waldenses, whom they now called heretics. Anyone who joined the pope's army would receive rewards beyond their wildest expectations. In exchange, the church would sometimes cancel the debts or taxes that people may have owed the government. The church often agreed to forgive criminals of crimes they had committed and promised that any money, cattle, or land that they stole could be theirs.

The armies grew quickly with the promise of such rewards. Soon they were on their way up into the mountain valleys, where they attacked and burned the settlements of the Waldenses.

> **The Waldenses always carried pages from the Bible in case they should meet someone who might want to hear truth.**

Crops were destroyed and herds of cattle and sheep stolen. Men, women, and children were executed.

As the news of these attacks spread, many of the Waldenses fled up higher into the mountains to hide in the forests and caves. For a while, it seemed that this refuge would be their home, a place of safety for their families. Once again, they taught their young people to be faithful to God and to spread the gospel as missionaries.

However, the armies of the church followed them there, too. Whole villages of Waldensian Christians were sometimes chased to the mouths of caves in which they had hidden. Then, trapped in the caves with no way of escape, they were suffocated with smoke from fires that their enemies lit at the entrance to the caves.

Before long the settlements of the Waldenses were being attacked and burned.

The Waldenses sometimes escaped through snowy mountain passes in the dead of winter. Sometimes God helped whole villages of men, women, and children sneak past armed sentries posted to prevent their escape.

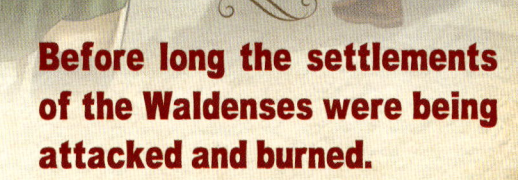

The stories of the heroic Waldenses and their faithfulness to God are an inspiration to us today. Sometimes God protected them and miraculously prevented them from being destroyed. Other times He allowed them to be martyred as witnesses for their faith.

The lives that were given for Jesus helped sow the seeds of the gospel for years to come.

The lives that were given for Jesus helped sow the seeds of the gospel for years to come. Often those who saw the horrible things that the church was doing to the Waldenses were inspired to stand up for God and take the Bible as the inspired Word of God.

Someday soon, Jesus will come, and then we will meet the Waldenses who stood faithfully for Him. They will receive a crown of life because they loved and obeyed Jesus even at the cost of their own lives.

We too can have a crown of life if we are faithful and obedient just like the Waldenses.

Our Prayer:

"Dear Jesus, I know that it would be difficult for me to suffer hardships such as those that the Waldenses did, but I know that You could help me do it. I pray that I will always be as faithful to You as they were."

Hidden Treasure Questions:

✓ If you had been living among the Waldenses, in what ways would you have shared the gospel with the world?

✓ Before Jesus comes again, God's people will go through some of the same kinds of trials that the Waldenses experienced. Will you be as true to Jesus as these faithful people were?

Listen to this story online!

Scan for bonus content

John Wycliffe

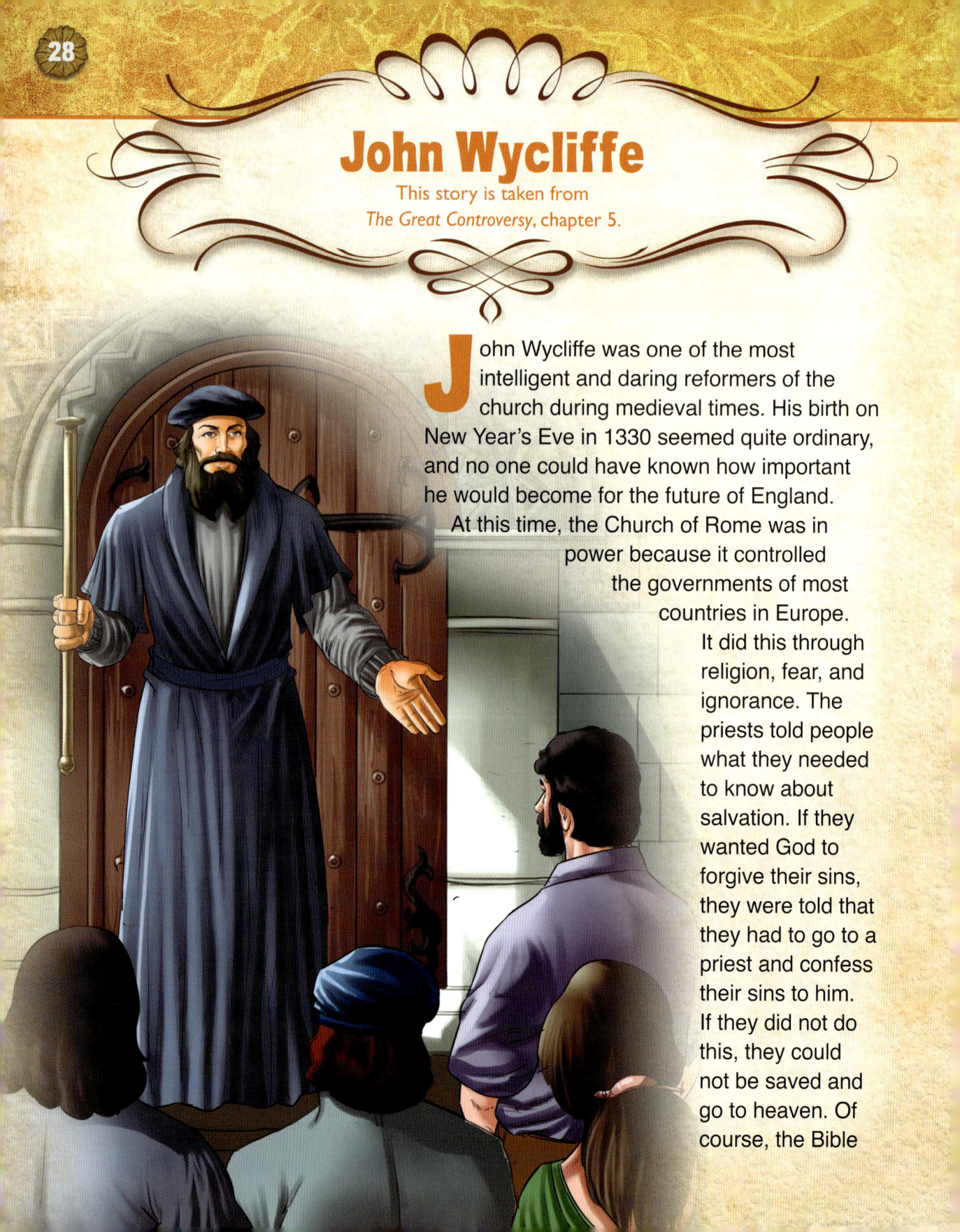

This story is taken from
The Great Controversy, chapter 5.

John Wycliffe was one of the most intelligent and daring reformers of the church during medieval times. His birth on New Year's Eve in 1330 seemed quite ordinary, and no one could have known how important he would become for the future of England. At this time, the Church of Rome was in power because it controlled the governments of most countries in Europe. It did this through religion, fear, and ignorance. The priests told people what they needed to know about salvation. If they wanted God to forgive their sins, they were told that they had to go to a priest and confess their sins to him. If they did not do this, they could not be saved and go to heaven. Of course, the Bible teaches no such thing, but no one knew it because they didn't have an opportunity to read the Bible for themselves.

In those days, there were no Bibles in the languages of the common people. John knew that superstition and fear were big problems among the people of his country because they had not been correctly taught about God.

So he decided that with God's help he would give the people of England a Bible in their own language. To do this, he needed to translate the Bible from the Latin language in which it was written at the time. It took him and his followers more than two years to finish their translation of the Bible, which was called the Wycliffe Bible.

John didn't know it, but his work as a translator would influence others in Europe to do the same thing for their countries. He has been called the "morning star of the Reformation," because he was one of the first to stand up against all the wrong things that he could see the church doing.

For example, he did not think that the church should have power over the governments of countries. He felt that the church should be a religious authority, but nothing more. John said that the Bible should be read and interpreted by individuals and not the church, as everybody was doing in those days.

He also taught that people were holy because God made them holy, not because they happened to be a monk, priest, or bishop. He told church leaders that it was wrong to use God's money to live lives of luxury and extravagance.

One of the things that John criticized most about the church in Rome was the traveling monks, known as church friars. These friars were lazy and didn't really do much work. The only thing they did was to collect money for the church by begging. They were also given the power to grant pardons for sins and even crimes by selling something they called indulgences.

If a person paid enough money, he would be given an indulgence, which was a piece of paper that could give forgiveness for any sin in the

> **John needed to translate the Bible from the Latin language in which it was written at the time.**

past, present, or future. This practice made the church very corrupt and England a dangerous place in which to live. Sometimes criminals were even released from prison and given these indulgences if they would go to fight in the pope's army.

By exposing the church in this way, John Wycliffe became one of the greatest enemies of the Church of Rome. He was taken to trial by the church three times, but the bishops could not stand up to his arguments from the Bible. At one trial, he said, "With whom do you think you are dealing? An old man on the brink of the grave? No, you are dealing with truth which is stronger than you, and it will overcome you."

Once when he was very sick and everyone thought that he was going to die, the priests and friars came to "pray" for him and give him his "last rites." That was something religious leaders in those days did to make sure that a person's soul was ready to go to heaven. The friars asked John to recant or give up all the things that he had said against the church so that he could go to heaven instead of hell.

But John got very angry when he heard this. "I will not die!" he told them. "God will raise me up to do even greater things for Him."

And He did. God helped him in a great spiritual revival that spread everywhere. His writings even influenced John Huss of Bohemia to begin a great reformation in that country against the corrupt Church of Rome. By God's grace, the "morning star of the Reformation" had made his mark in England, and Europe was never the same.

> John taught that people were holy because God made them holy.

Our Prayer:

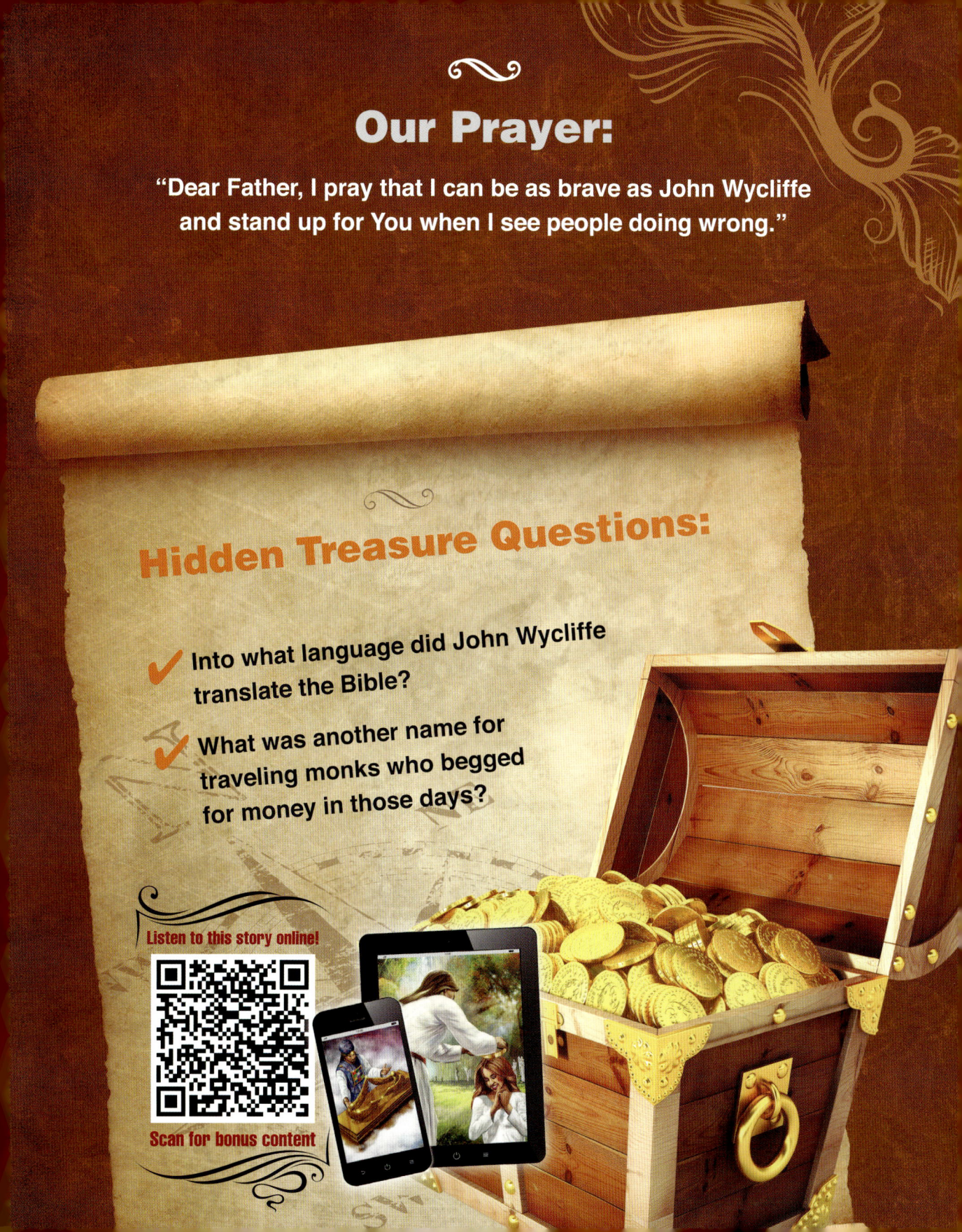

"Dear Father, I pray that I can be as brave as John Wycliffe and stand up for You when I see people doing wrong."

Hidden Treasure Questions:

✓ Into what language did John Wycliffe translate the Bible?

✓ What was another name for traveling monks who begged for money in those days?

Listen to this story online!

Scan for bonus content

Huss and Jerome

This story is taken from
The Great Controversy, chapter 6.

John Huss was born into a poor family in Bohemia in 1369. While he was still young, his father died. This made it difficult for the family, but his mother insisted that John should study. This he did, and God blessed him. Eventually he was able to go to the University of Prague because someone paid his expenses.

He studied hard and graduated with honors. He was faithful to God, and everybody was impressed with his gentle personality. After graduation, he entered the priesthood, went to work for the king, got a job as a professor, and then finally became president of the university.

About this time, a man named Jerome returned from England with some writings of John Wycliffe. Huss read these writings and was soon questioning many things that the Church of Rome was doing and teaching.

Then two strangers arrived in Prague from England to preach against the corrupt teachings of the church. However, church leaders forced them to stop speaking publicly. So since both were artists, they painted two pictures on a wall along a main street in town.

One picture showed Jesus humbly coming into Jerusalem riding on a donkey. He and His disciples were dressed in the simple clothes of poor men. The other picture showed the pope dressed in his rich robes and three-tiered crown riding on a horse that was magnificently decorated. Trumpeters marched in front of him, and following him were cardinals and bishops dressed in dazzling clothes and jewels.

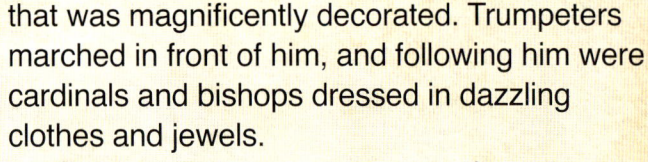

These pictures were a sermon that no one could argue with because it showed the real differences between the pope and Jesus. These pictures made John Huss see the Church of Rome in a new light, and he began to study the Bible even more. When he criticized the church in his university classes, the church leaders asked many of his students to leave town. However, these students took the message with them to

> **By now Pope Gregory VII was very angry with John Huss and called him to Rome for a trial.**

Germany and other countries in Europe. So the punishment that was given to stop the message was the very thing that caused it to spread.

By now Pope Gregory VII was very angry and called John Huss to Rome for a trial. However, the king and university officials in Prague didn't want him to go, because they knew that he would probably be executed.

The pope condemned Huss as a heretic and banned him from the church. A heretic was someone who was talking against the church and the government. Then the church leaders announced that heaven was now closed to everyone in the city of Prague. That was a lie, because only God decides who goes to heaven, not the church or the pope.

This frightened the people in Prague, because they had always been taught that the pope spoke for God on earth. Many people blamed John Huss for all the troubles and demanded that he be sent to Rome as a prisoner.

So Huss left Prague to avoid further trouble, but his travels gave him a chance to preach far and wide. Soon his message was helping to start a religious reformation in other places.

When things calmed down in Prague, Huss returned to the university. He was joined by Jerome, who had brought him the writings of Wycliffe. There they worked together to preach the truth and to show the people that the church was going against the Bible.

But trouble was brewing. The city officials arrested John and put him on trial as a heretic against Rome. When he was asked to admit that what he had taught was wrong, he said, "I call God to witness that what I have written and preached has been only to rescue souls for heaven." Then the church leaders began to persecute Jerome for his friendship with Huss. They put him in prison, too. He was not as brave as Huss. Because he was scared, he said that he had been wrong in what he was teaching. However, afterward, when he realized what he had done, Jerome humbly confessed that he would rather die than deny Jesus again.

"Prove to me from the Bible that I am wrong, and I will give up everything I have said against the church," he told them.

But the church leaders of Rome couldn't prove him wrong. So they condemned him to be burned at the stake, just as they had John Huss.

The influence of Huss and Jerome helped the people in Bohemia see that the Bible was the most important book in the world. And soon the Protestant Reformation was growing by leaps and bounds all across Europe.

What a great message for us today. We have to be faithful to Jesus no matter what. We need to stand for truth, and the only way we can do that is to pray and study the Bible every day.

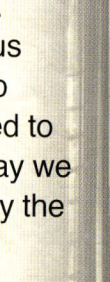

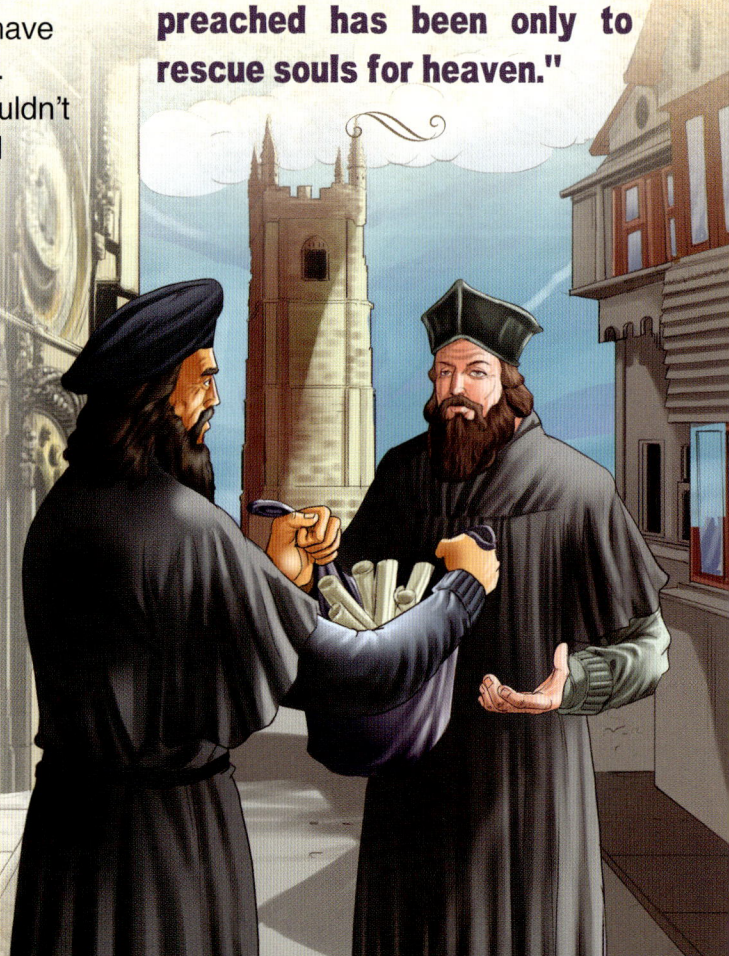

> "I call God to witness that what I have written and preached has been only to rescue souls for heaven."

Our Prayer:

"Dear Jesus, I want to be faithful to You and the truths in the Bible when hard times come."

Hidden Treasure Questions:

- ✓ When the two artists painted a picture on a wall, it made the pope angry. Why?
- ✓ What were the names of the two reformers in Bohemia who were burned at the stake?

Listen to this story online!

Scan for bonus content

Martin Luther as a Young Man

This story is taken from
The Great Controversy, chapter 7.

Martin Luther pulled his black-hooded cape down around his shoulders to keep out the rain. Lightning flashed all around him as he dodged this way and that, trying to avoid the mud puddles. Thunder boomed overhead, making him jump now and then, and he realized that walking in such a storm could be dangerous.

He had been at his father's house in Mansfield that day and was now on his way back to the University of Erfurt in Germany. Martin had recently completed his master's degree and was now getting another degree in law. At age 21, he was being urged by his father to get married to a young woman from a wealthy family, but Martin wasn't ready for marriage. Lately he had been thinking of becoming a monk in the Roman Catholic Church, which was something many parents wished for their children.

The day had been a hot one, and heavy rains were coming down as though a faucet had been opened above Martin in the blackened sky. Suddenly a streak of lightning hit the ground next to him, throwing him violently into the mud. "Help me, St. Anne!" he cried out in fear to one of his favorite Catholic saints. "For this, I will become a monk."

Martin lay on the ground stunned for several moments, and then finally got to his feet. The rain was still coming down, drenching him to the skin, but he didn't care. He was glad to be alive.

The year was 1505, and it proved to be a turning point for Martin. Until now he had not been a very spiritual person, but his experience in the rainstorm made him realize that everyone is just one step away from death. Now he decided to give himself to religious studies and the service of God. His father was not happy about this, but Martin went through with it anyway.

He had come from a poor family. As a boy, he was often hungry because there was nothing to eat in the house. Sometimes he had to go singing door-to-door to beg for his food. His father and mother felt bad about the family's poverty, but somehow they managed to send all of their children to school. They believed that education was the answer for a better life, and Martin came to believe it too.

Martin was very smart and loved to study, but his teachers taught him many ideas about God that were not true. They filled his mind with superstitious teachings about witches, devils, and the horrors of hellfire. He was taught that the only way to be saved was to confess his sins to a priest, to buy holy candles from the church, and to pray to the saints for mercy.

He did not know that Jesus' death on the cross had already paid the price for his sins and that all he needed to do was ask Jesus to forgive his sins. Confessing his sins to a priest would not save him because the priests were sinners too.

Suddenly a streak of lightning hit the ground next to him, throwing him violently into the mud.

By the time he had entered the university, friends of the family were helping to pay Martin's school expenses, so he was much better off financially. But he still struggled with his doubts about who God was and what God expected of him. He wanted to be a good person; he just didn't know how to give up all the wrong ideas that he had been taught about the Bible.

By now Luther could read and write many languages. One of the languages he learned that helped him better understand the Bible was Latin. In Martin's day all Bibles were written in Latin, an old language from the days of the ancient Roman Empire. So if a person couldn't read Latin, he couldn't read the Bible.

However, the Holy Spirit was beginning to open Martin's mind to new ideas. God was with him, and he now began to discover the power of prayer. Praying could help him get closer to God. It could help him have peace in his heart.

But Martin knew that he needed more than just prayer. He needed to study the Bible. Unfortunately, Bibles were scarce in those days. He did not own one and had never even seen a complete Bible. He had seen only a few verses and chapters of Scripture at a time.

Martin did not know it, but his desire to study the Bible was opening a whole new chapter in his life.

Sometimes Luther had to go singing door-to-door to beg for his food. His father and mother felt bad about the family's poverty.

Our Prayer:

"Thank You, Jesus, for forgiving my sins and making me as white as snow with the robe of Your righteousness."

Hidden Treasure Questions:

- ✓ What should you do if Satan tempts you to think that you are too bad for Jesus to love?

- ✓ What can you do to help others know that Jesus died to save them from their sins?

Listen to this story online!

Scan for bonus content

Martin and the Scary Staircase

This story is taken from *The Great Controversy*, chapter 7 and based on Romans 1:17.

Martin Luther was studying to be a priest, but he struggled with doubts about his life as a Christian. When he discovered the power of prayer, it began to change his life. Then he made another great discovery that would change the world.

One day he found a complete copy of the Bible chained to a pulpit in the library at the University of Erfurt in Germany. In reverence and awe, he turned the sacred pages and read the wonderful verses that he had never before seen.

"If God would give me a complete Bible of my own, I would be the happiest man alive," he said. Angels were by his side to encourage him with such thoughts and to inspire him to study more. Now whenever he had the chance, he came back to the library to study the precious pages of the Bible.

Martin Luther wanted to understand the Bible better, but he still struggled with a deep sense of his sinfulness. He entered a monastery and continued to study. He had been told that if he prayed and fasted enough or went without sleep, God would accept him. If he beat himself with a whip to pay for his sins, maybe God would not burn him too long in the fires of hell. None of these strange beliefs brought him peace of mind. None of them made him feel as though God could ever love or forgive him.

Then one day Dr. Staupitz, a fellow priest in the university, came to visit Martin. He could see that Martin was very sad. Martin told him about the horrible struggles that he was having spiritually, and that he was almost ready to give up his studies as a priest.

Dr. Staupitz explained that Martin should not torture himself about all the bad things he had done in his life. Instead, he should give them all to Jesus. "Trust in God," he said. "And let the righteousness of Jesus cover your sins."

From that day forward, Martin was a changed man. Dr. Staupitz urged him to preach on Sundays, and soon he found that he had a hidden talent. He spoke with such power and conviction that people began coming to Sunday services regularly just to hear him preach.

Then in 1510, Martin decided to make a pilgrimage to Rome, the capital city of the Holy Roman Empire. It had been a lifelong dream of his to see Rome, and now he made the journey on foot, walking more than 800 miles to accomplish it. Along the way, he stopped overnight at monasteries to rest and then continued on his way each morning.

When he finally arrived in Rome, he fell on his knees to thank God for this opportunity to visit the historic city. In his mind, this was the most holy place on earth. In fact, he called it "Holy Rome." However, he was astonished and disappointed by all that he heard and saw! Most of the leaders of the church were not spiritual, and actually were very rude at times, even making fun of God during Sunday morning mass.

One day he found a complete copy of the Bible chained to a pulpit.

Martin was so discouraged that he decided to have a special session of prayer at a place in Rome called the *Scala Sancta*, or Pilate's staircase. The pope had said that he would give an indulgence, which was a certificate of forgiveness, to anyone who could climb the 28 marble stairsteps on their knees in prayer.

Martin went to the staircase early one morning and began the painful task of climbing the steps on his knees, offering a prayer on each step. He was partway up the stairs when suddenly he thought he heard a voice as loud as thunder say, "The just shall live by faith!" He was shocked and even frightened by the voice, and wondered if this might be God speaking to him. The words were from Romans 1:17. Those words made him seriously think about why he was climbing these steps.

He had always thought that doing such things would make him more holy, but he couldn't believe that anymore. The message he had just heard was clear. God was making it plain that our works cannot save us. Only our faith in God will save us.

Remembering the words of Dr. Staupitz, Martin jumped up in shame and ran down the stairs, never to return. Loud and clear was the message to his heart that day. He realized now how pointless were the many things that he had been doing to earn salvation. He understood clearly that we can do nothing to make ourselves more holy before God, but "if we confess our sins, He is faithful and just to forgive us our sins and to cleanse us from all unrighteousness" (1 John 1:9). Only the blood of Jesus can cover our sins. Only His robe of righteousness will make us as white as snow.

> **Martin went to the staircase early one morning and began to climb the steps on his knees, offering a prayer on each step.**

Our Prayer:

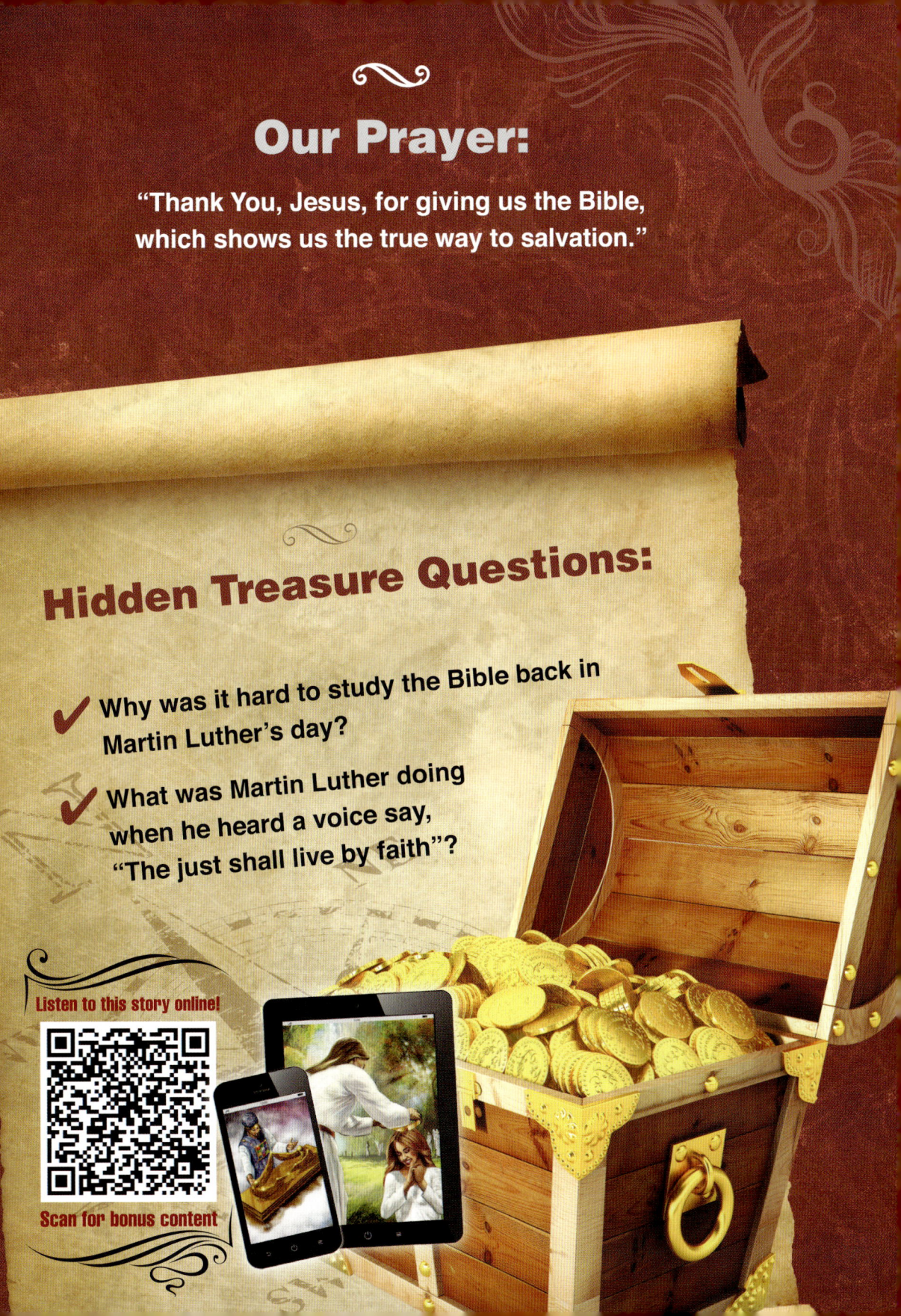

"Thank You, Jesus, for giving us the Bible, which shows us the true way to salvation."

Hidden Treasure Questions:

✓ Why was it hard to study the Bible back in Martin Luther's day?

✓ What was Martin Luther doing when he heard a voice say, "The just shall live by faith"?

Listen to this story online!

Scan for bonus content

Martin Luther Goes to Court

This story is taken from
The Great Controversy, chapters 7 and 8.

Luther's life had changed so much because of the wonderful things that he had found in the Bible. Now he wanted others to know about them too. He was not happy about all the things he saw that were wrong in the Church of Rome, because they didn't help people get closer to Jesus or bring glory to God.

Therefore, he decided to write a statement telling everyone all the things the church taught that did not agree with the Bible. He put them on a large piece of paper and called them the "95 Theses." To make sure that everyone saw the statement, he nailed it to the church door where he was a professor at the University of Wittenberg.

This happened in the year 1517, and it was big news in those days because no one spoke against the church such as he had. If anyone did, then they were punished. But Luther didn't care. "I love the church," he said. "However, the Bible comes first. If the church doesn't agree with that, then they must change."

For example, Martin said that according to the Bible people should not have to confess their sins to a priest. They should be able to pray to God and tell Him their problems. He also said that it was wrong for the church to sell indulgences. Indulgences were pieces of paper that people could buy that said they could be forgiven of the sins they committed.

The church leaders would tell people that old relics, such as Jesus' cross or little bottles of the tears of Mary, should be worshipped. Martin Luther did not believe this. He also said that it was wrong for the church leaders to say that there was a temporary state of punishment called purgatory. The church was teaching that if people gave enough money, they could get other people out of that horrible place called purgatory. Once again, that was a church teaching. It was not from the Bible.

> **To make sure that everyone saw the statement, Luther nailed it to the church door.**

Of course, the leaders in Rome were not happy with Martin Luther for the things that he was saying against the pope and the church. They made a lot of money because of these teachings and tried many ways to get Luther to stop. But God protected him and kept him safe. Also at this time, Luther's thoughtful young friend Philipp Melanchthon was a great source of calming encouragement to him.

Finally, the pope and other leaders in Rome said that Martin Luther needed to be tried in court for all of the things that he was saying against the church. Charles V had just been crowned the new emperor in Germany, and the church felt he should be the one to bring Luther to trial. The trial was to be held in a city in Germany called Worms. Martin's friends were afraid that he might be attacked and killed by his enemies on the way, but King Charles guaranteed his safety. So Martin made the trip to Worms.

He was now very famous for all the things he had been saying against the church. People all over Europe had read Martin's "95 Theses" because of a new invention called the printing press. They liked Martin, and although most of them were afraid of offending the church, they agreed with him. The church was very corrupt and needed to change.

On the way to the trial, the people lined the streets to cheer for him. Every town he traveled through was crowded with people who wanted to see this well-known priest of the Catholic Church.

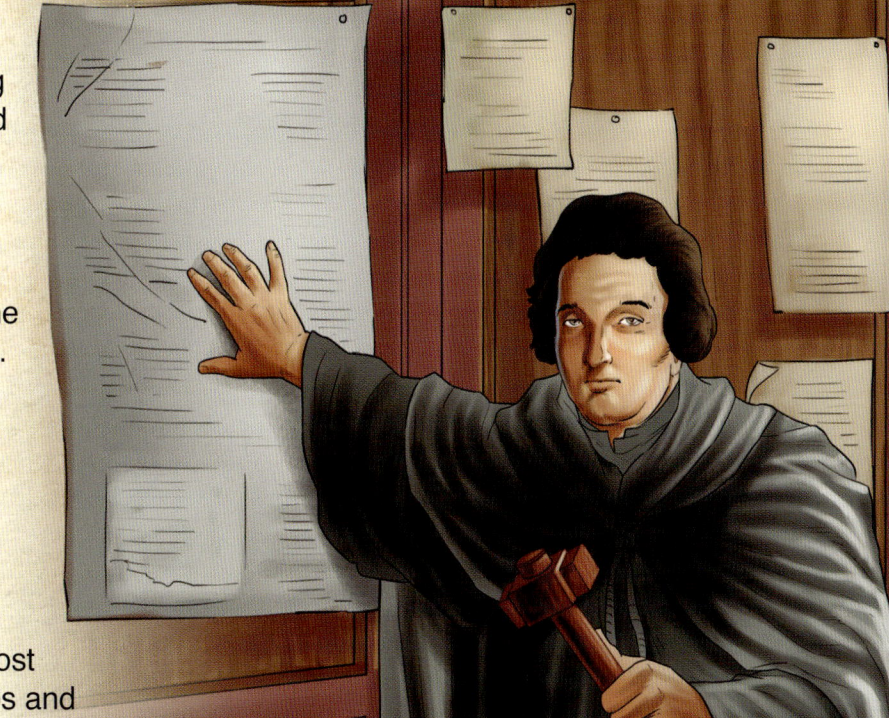

The trial at Worms was attended by the most powerful church bishops and cardinals, who were dressed in their fancy robes and expensive

jewels. Their goal was to get Luther to recant and retract the things that he had said about the church. To "recant" meant that he was wrong and sorry for all the things that he had said. And to "retract" meant that he would have to take back everything that he had written against the church.

If the church leaders could not convince him to do this, he would be pronounced a heretic. Then he would be executed for heresy because of his attacks on the Church of Rome. A heretic was anyone who used the Bible to teach that the church was wrong.

But Martin was not sorry for the things that he had said, because he said they were all true. "I cannot and will not retract," he said bravely. "Here I stand, I can do no other; may God help me."

The emperor of Germany did not agree with Martin Luther, as many had hoped he would. But most of the princes in Germany did. So Martin was allowed to live and went on to translate the Bible into German. This inspired others to translate the Bible into their own languages, too.

Soon everyone was reading the Bible for themselves, and because of this there was a great religious revival. They were learning that God is not a cruel, vengeful God waiting to punish the sinner. He is a kind, loving God who wants us to turn back to Him and spend forever in heaven, where He has a place prepared for all who love Him.

The trial at Worms was attended by the most powerful bishops and cardinals, who were dressed in their fancy robes and expensive jewels.

Our Prayer:

"Dear God, thank You for sending Martin Luther to help us see the Bible in a new way."

Hidden Treasure Questions:

✓ What were some of the things that the church was teaching that Martin Luther said were wrong?

✓ What was the name of the city where Martin Luther had to go to trial?

Listen to this story online!

Scan for bonus content

Revival in Switzerland

This story is taken from *The Great Controversy*, chapter 9.

Ulric Zwingli was born in a peasant's cottage in the Swiss Alps. His father was a poor village magistrate, but he wanted his son to get an education. So the boy was sent away to boarding school at an early age. He was a brilliant child, and before long, it was hard to find teachers who could keep up with him.

When he was still a young man, the church friars wanted him to become a monk because he was already a very good speaker and writer. However, Zwingli's father heard about the plans of the friars and refused to let his son join that "lazy bunch of beggars."

His father then sent him to Basel, and it was there that Zwingli first discovered that God's grace was free. Salvation could not be bought and sold, as the church was teaching.

When he was hired to be a preacher in Zurich, Switzerland, he was told that he could minister to only the rich, important people. However, he told the church leaders that he planned to help anyone who needed him, just as Jesus had done.

Soon people heard about him and began flocking to his church every Sunday morning. Government leaders and educated scholars crowded in along with poor peasants to hear his unusual sermons from the gospels of Jesus. Before long, the church was full every week with standing room only.

Then some of Martin Luther's writings were sent to Zwingli from Germany, and he realized there were others in Europe who were thinking the same as he was. One thing he began to preach against was the sale of indulgences. These pieces of paper were sold everywhere by the church, and they were promising people that any sin could be forgiven for a price. In other words, salvation could be bought.

Like Wycliffe, Huss, and Luther, Zwingli hated this custom and taught that selling indulgences was an evil thing. His message was so well received in Zurich that when an officer from Rome came selling the indulgences, he was met at the town gate and told to move on.

In 1519, a terrible epidemic swept through Switzerland, and Zwingli himself became very sick. Many predicted that he would die, but God healed him, and he became an even greater preacher. His message was always the same: Faith in Jesus' sacrifice and His righteousness is the only way to get eternal life.

Of course, this was opposite from what the state church was teaching, and it made a lot of trouble for him with the Church of Rome. A date was set for a church council to condemn Zwingli for all the things that he had said against it. It was to be held in the city of Baden, but the government leaders in Zurich would not let Zwingli go. They had seen many reformers burned at the stake by church leaders and were afraid the same thing might happen to him after the trial.

A church officer from Rome named Eck came to the council in Baden dressed in fine robes and glittering jewels. Zwingli's students came to represent him, but they were dressed in the simple clothes of common folks.

The students were not allowed to take notes during the meetings, which lasted many

Soon people heard about him and began flocking to his church every Sunday morning.

days. However, every morning they came with Bible verses ready to answer Eck's arguments from the previous day. The officers of Rome wondered, "How did they manage this? How can they be so eloquent when they have no real training as debaters in a court of law?"

What Eck didn't know was that every evening after the council the students would write down everything that had been said that day. Then they would take the notes to Zurich 16 miles away, where Zwingli lived. Zwingli would read the notes that night, and then write letters of advice as to how his students should answer the arguments made by Eck. These letters were then smuggled past the guards at the gates and back into Baden the next morning by students who carried baskets of chickens on their heads.

> **These letters were then smuggled past the guards by students who carried baskets of chickens on their heads.**

The church council continued for 18 days, and when it was finished, Eck and his group of church officers said that they had won. Zwingli and his followers were excommunicated from the church. And according to the Church of Rome, they would never be allowed to go to heaven. Of course, this was not true, because only Jesus holds the keys to heaven.

Now, in spite of all that the Church in Rome had done to stop Zwingli and his followers, the revival in Switzerland only grew stronger. Soon after the church council in Baden, the churches in Bern and Basel officially separated from the Church of Rome.

Our Prayer:

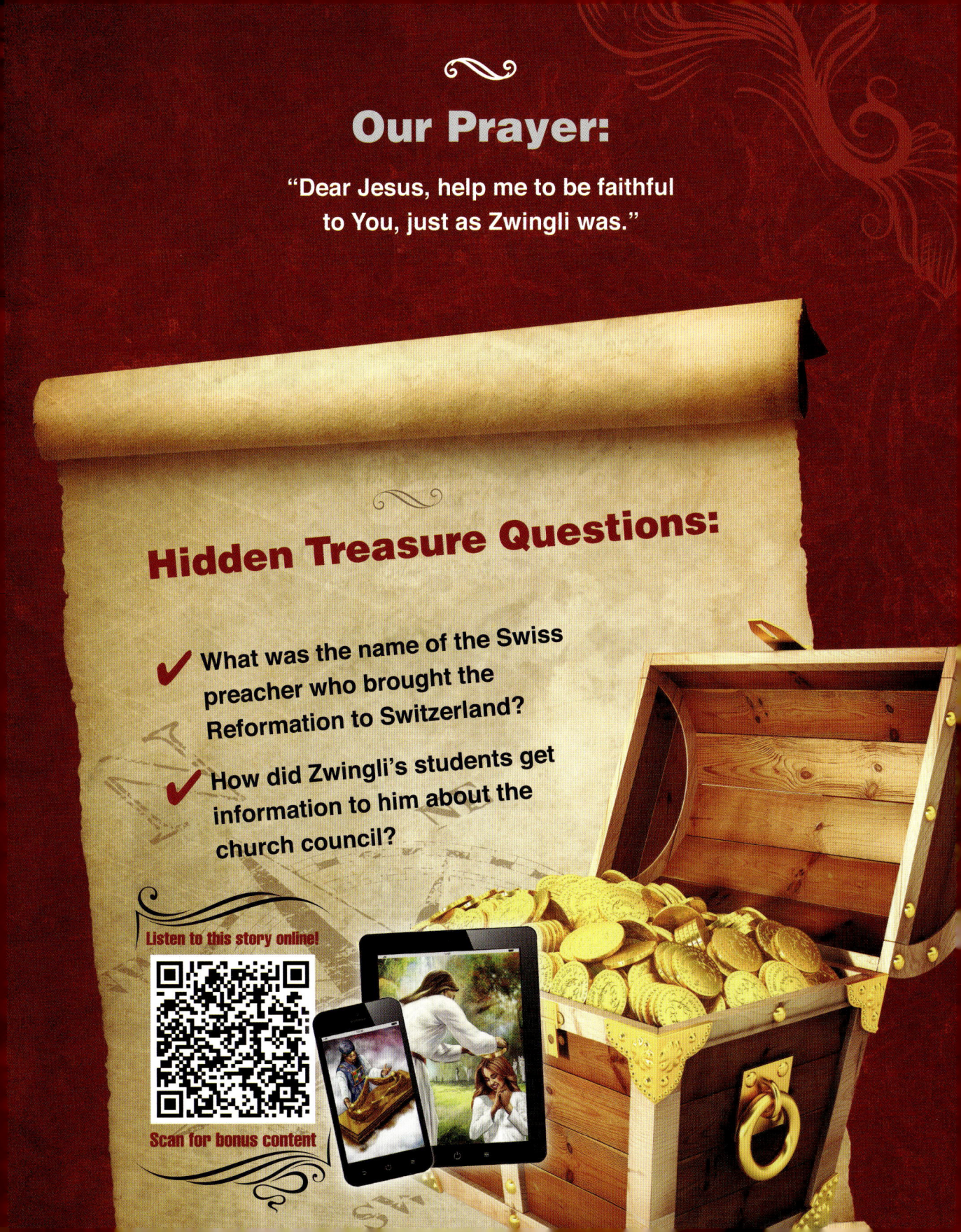

"Dear Jesus, help me to be faithful to You, just as Zwingli was."

Hidden Treasure Questions:

✓ What was the name of the Swiss preacher who brought the Reformation to Switzerland?

✓ How did Zwingli's students get information to him about the church council?

Listen to this story online!

Scan for bonus content

The French Reformation

This story is taken from *The Great Controversy*, chapter 12.

The Reformation in Germany struggled to move forward against the Church of Rome, but things were not going well for the reformers. Because the government leaders would not stand up against the church, severe persecution followed. Many reformers gave their lives as martyrs and died.

Switzerland suffered too, and religious persecution led to civil war there. Zwingli and many other reformers died when government forces attacked them in Zurich.

In France, the light of the Reformation was also breaking as dawn on the country. Lefevre, who was an old professor at the University of Paris, was doing research on the history of saints and martyrs in the church. He began reading the Bible to get information for his research and made some discoveries that did not agree with what the Church of Rome taught about the worship of saints.

He realized that we should not be worshipping the saints, because they were not in heaven. They were dead. This opened his eyes to the fact that the church was being corrupt just to get money, and it made him angry and disgusted.

Lefevre and Farel, one of his students at the university, introduced the king and queen of France to the gospel of the Protestant Reformation. Then Lefevre translated the New Testament of the Bible into French, and the head bishop in town made sure that everyone got a copy. This brought about some amazing changes in the community of Meaux, France, because every day the number of Protestant Christians grew.

However, Satan was not happy, and soon he brought back the persecution that had been used by the church for centuries. Many were burned at the stake for their faith in God, but the blood of the martyrs became the seed of the church. As people watched the Protestants so bravely give their lives for Jesus, they decided that they would join the ranks too.

Then a new kind of reformer arrived to kindle the fires of the Reformation. His name was Louis Berquin, and he was a different story altogether! He was born into a family of nobles and became a fashionable knight at court. He loved the Church of Rome, but God guided him to the Bible. In the Bible, he learned that people didn't need to confess to a priest. They could pray to Jesus. Only Jesus could forgive their sins, and people shouldn't have to pay money for their sins to be forgiven. Berquin realized that the Church

Lefevre translated the New Testament of the Bible into French, and everyone got a copy.

of Rome taught none of these amazing truths, so he decided that he must give up his loyalty to the pope.

Soon he was preaching everywhere condemning the pope, and this made him a great enemy of the church. "He is worse than Martin Luther!" the leaders in Rome said, and they put him in prison three different times. However, the king of France would always let him out.

When church leaders challenged Berquin about his beliefs, the king asked them to defend their arguments with the Bible. But their lies could not be supported by the Bible. The only weapons that they knew how to use were prison, torture, and burning people at the stake.

When an image of Mary was damaged in the streets of Paris, the monks stirred up a riot and blamed Berquin for the broken image.

He was tried and condemned to death. They carried out his sentence the same day, because they were afraid that his friends might try to rescue him.

Berquin went bravely to his death, courageously standing as a witness for the gospel and for Jesus, who is the King of kings. They marched him through the streets, but no tears

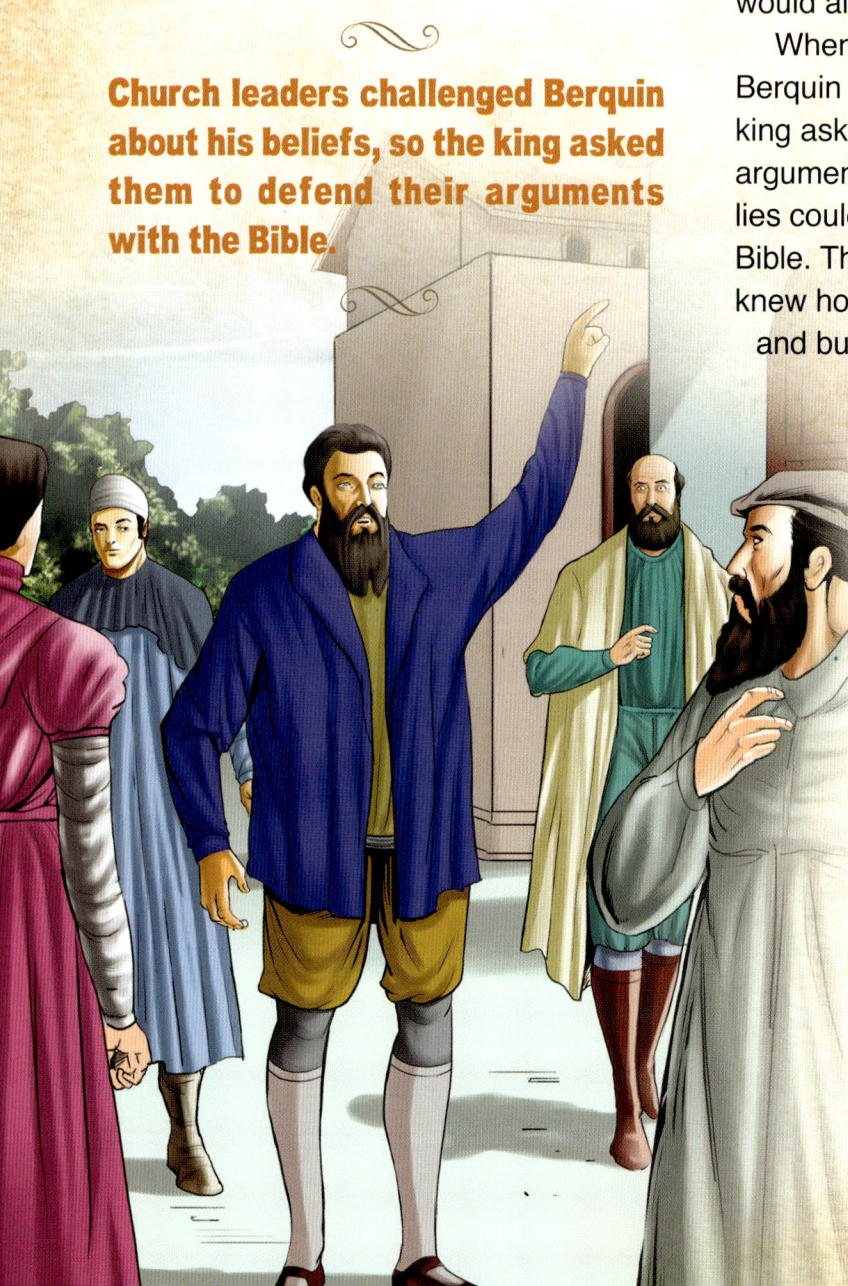

Church leaders challenged Berquin about his beliefs, so the king asked them to defend their arguments with the Bible.

came to his eyes. The peace of heaven was on his face, and when they lit the wood piled around him, he was not afraid to die. He knew Jesus, who has the keys of death and is alive forevermore (Revelation 1:18).

Many who witnessed his death were inspired to stand for Jesus too. "We are ready to die cheerfully for Jesus as Berquin has done," they said, "because we have set our eyes on the life that is to come."

John Calvin was another famous French reformer, but he had been educated to be a priest. As a young man, he was very loyal to the Church of Rome. A cousin of his who was a Protestant reformer came to Paris, and the two of them always had something to talk about.

"There are two kinds of religions," his cousin said one day. "One religion is something that man has invented to save himself by ceremonies and all the good things he does. The other religion is what we find revealed in the Bible, which teaches men to look for salvation through the grace of God."

Calvin refused to listen to such arguments. "I'll have none of those new teachings!" he said. "I refuse to believe that I have been living a lie all my life."

However, alone in his bedroom at night he would think about what his cousin had said, and it troubled him. He knew that he was a sinner and realized that his religion had no real Savior to save him.

One day while passing through a public marketplace, he witnessed the execution of a Christian heretic. He was so impressed with the expression of peace on the martyr's face that he decided that he needed whatever it was the martyr had.

So he began to study his Bible seriously and found Jesus. "Lord, You have placed Your Word before me like a torch and touched my heart," he prayed humbly, seeing for the first time the meaning of the Christian gospel.

Now he spent his time going from house to house in city after city preaching and teaching the Word of God. He was so successful that people everywhere wanted to hear the gospel.

About this time, a spiritual revival swept through Paris, and though the Church of Rome didn't like it, the king allowed it to go on. He even opened his biggest churches to hear the Protestants preach. People in Paris were curious about the message that the Protestants brought.

Unfortunately, most of them rejected it and went back to worship in the Catholic churches. But trouble was coming. One night friends came to warn Calvin that his life was in danger, and he barely escaped by climbing out a window.

He fled to Geneva, Switzerland, and there he became a great preacher of the gospel, bringing the light of the Protestant Reformation to people everywhere.

Back in France the window of opportunity to preach the gospel had passed. Most people there had rejected the gospel, and now a great time of persecution began that was worse than anyone had ever seen before. Protestant Christians were arrested every day and executed as enemies of the Church of Rome. Hundreds were tortured and burned to death because they wouldn't give up their belief that only through Jesus could they be saved.

No one felt safe any longer in France. Even people who weren't Protestants felt that they must leave. Thousands of the brightest, best-educated, and most skilled people now fled.

Unfortunately, France never recovered from the terrible treatment they gave the Protestants, and more than two centuries later they would pay the price during the French Revolution.

Berquin went bravely to his death, courageously standing as a witness for the gospel.

Our Prayer:

"Dear Father, help me to be faithful to You, even if it should cost me my life."

Hidden Treasure Questions:

✓ How did Louis Berquin die?

✓ What made John Calvin decide to become a Protestant preacher?

Listen to this story online!

Scan for bonus content

Bow or Burn at the Stake

This story is taken from
The Great Controversy, chapter 13.

The light of the gospel came to the countries of northern Europe, too. Missionary travelers came on foot to spread the good news of God's Word. The Waldensian Bible was translated into Dutch. This gave the people a chance to read the gospel story for themselves.

But Charles V, who was emperor over much of Europe, did not believe in religious freedom. For years, he tried to stamp out the work of the reformers who would preach the good news of the gospel. The Church of Rome knew that if the Protestants were not stopped, the church would lose its power over the people.

It was considered a crime for common people to read the Bible. If they preached or even listened to the gospel, they could receive the death penalty. Praying to God in secret was not allowed, and neither was singing a psalm. If a Christian refused to bow to an image of a saint in church, he could be burned at the stake.

Thousands died during Charles V's reign from 1516 until 1556. Whole families were executed together for their faith. One family that was brought to the place of execution because they had stayed home to worship instead of going to mass was very brave. When asked what they did when they worshipped at home, the youngest son said, "We fell on our knees and prayed that God would open our minds and pardon our sins. We prayed that our king's reign would be prosperous and his life happy." Many were impressed by this testimony, but the father and his son were burned at the stake anyway.

Those were terrible times. Satan hated God so much that he would possess the minds of evil men and get them to cruelly persecute the people of God. He knew that the Protestant Christians were pointing people to Jesus, and that made Satan furious! There was nothing he wouldn't do to stop them.

But the rage of the persecutors was equaled by the faith of the martyrs. Young men and women stood courageously for God, even in death. Wives stood by their husbands as they were burned at the stake, and children sang and prayed for their executioners. It was said that those Protestant prisoners would go to their executions dressed in their best clothes, as if they were going to a wedding.

And as in the days of the early Christian church, the blood of the Christians became the seed of the church.

In Sweden, the gospel was better received. Two brothers became champions for God: Olaf and Laurentius Petri. Those two young men were sons of a blacksmith in the town of Orebro, but had studied under Martin Luther and Melanchthon in Germany. It was there that they learned to be great teachers of God's Word.

> **It was considered a crime for common people to read the Bible. If they preached or even listened to the gospel, they could receive the death penalty.**

Olaf was a fine speaker and was as full of enthusiasm as Luther. Laurentius was more like Melanchthon, calm and thoughtful. Wherever they went, troublemakers for the church followed behind them. Often evil priests would stir up the people in a town and turn them into a drunken mob. On several occasions Olaf barely escaped with his life. But the king liked Olaf and Laurentius and would sometimes send his soldiers to protect them.

The Church of Rome knew that as long as the people couldn't read, they would continue to be ignorant and superstitious. However, the king of Sweden was impressed with all that Olaf and Laurentius Petri had done for Sweden, and decided that he would become a Protestant Christian. With the power of God in his kingdom, he was sure his nation would be strong.

The king was determined that his nation would move forward with the gospel, but to do this he knew that he would have to have a copy of the Bible in his own language. There were no Bibles in the Swedish language at that time, so he asked Olaf and Laurentius to translate one.

When the translation was finished, he asked the ministers in his kingdom to preach from that Bible and to explain it to the people in their churches. Teachers were instructed to teach their students how to read and study the Bible.

As the king had hoped, the Bible changed his country for the better. Sweden became one of the strongest countries for Protestantism. It helped the people become honest, hardworking, godly men and women and pushed away the darkness of ignorance and superstition.

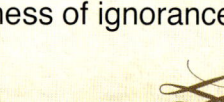

It was said that those Protestant prisoners would go to their executions dressed in their best clothes.

Our Prayer:

"Dear Jesus, many people have suffered taking the gospel of the Bible to the world. Help me to be willing to do that too, no matter the cost."

Hidden Treasure Questions:

- ✓ Who was the emperor for much of Europe from 1516 to 1556?

- ✓ What were the names of the two Swedish brothers who translated the Bible?

Listen to this story online!

Scan for bonus content

Tyndale the Translator

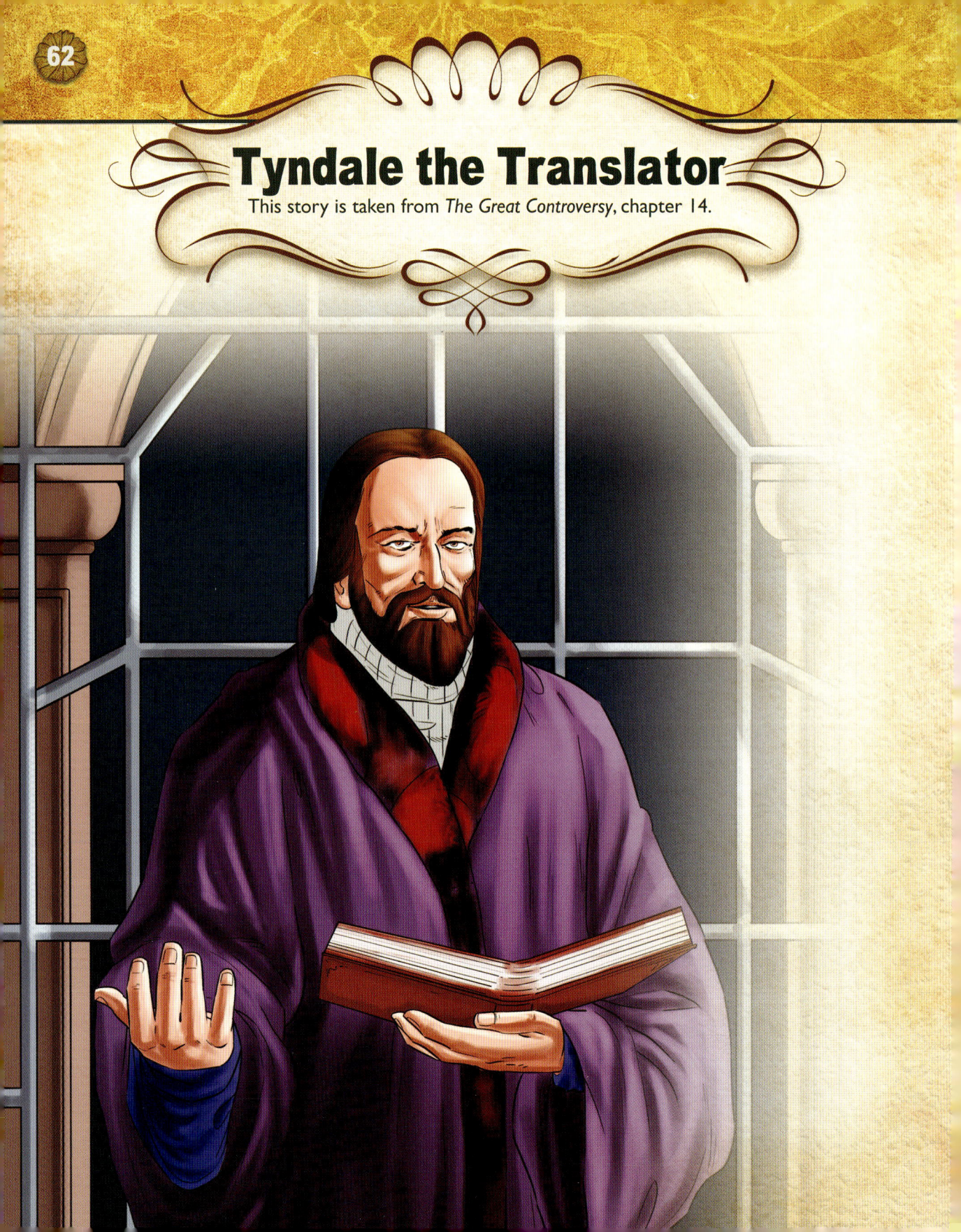

This story is taken from *The Great Controversy*, chapter 14.

The gospel was gaining ground in Europe because of all the work done by Protestant reformers. Many people were hearing the truth from the Bible as they never had before. In the 1380s, Wycliffe had pioneered the way in England by translating the Bible from Latin, a dead language that only the priests, monks, and bishops of the Church of Rome could read.

Wycliffe's Bible had not been printed at that time because the printing press was not invented until the 1400s. If people wanted copies of the Bible back then, it had to be copied by hand. Only the very rich could afford to buy such a Bible.

William Tyndale wished that he could translate the Bible into English so that everybody could afford it. More than anything, he wanted the common people to have the Bible to read in their own language.

Church leaders from Rome claimed that common people should not be reading the Bible. "The church has been given the Bible, and the church alone can explain it," they said.

Tyndale did not agree and courageously replied, "People don't need someone to interpret the Bible for them. God teaches His children to find their Father in His Word." Tyndale hoped that someday the Bible would be so common in England that a farm boy could know as much about the Bible as a preacher.

After studying Hebrew, Greek, and German, Tyndale went to work translating the Bible into English.

However, church leaders in the town where he lived didn't give him any peace. They persecuted him relentlessly until he finally fled to London. He worked there for a while, but again he was forced to flee. After the church leaders threatened to kill him, he finally fled to Germany.

In Germany, around the year 1525, Tyndale started printing his

William Tyndale wished that he could translate the Bible into English so that everybody could afford it.

first copies of the New Testament. Twice more he was forbidden to print, but that didn't stop him. When he was told that he could not print in one city, he simply moved to another city.

At last, in the city of Worms, where Luther had been put on trial, Tyndale was finally allowed to finish the project. He printed 3,000 copies of the New Testament. Friends of Tyndale managed to smuggle the books out of Worms, and they were circulated throughout London. The Word of God had won the battle. Those who had been waiting for copies in England rejoiced that God's Word was now available to them.

Tyndale printed 3,000 copies of the New Testament.

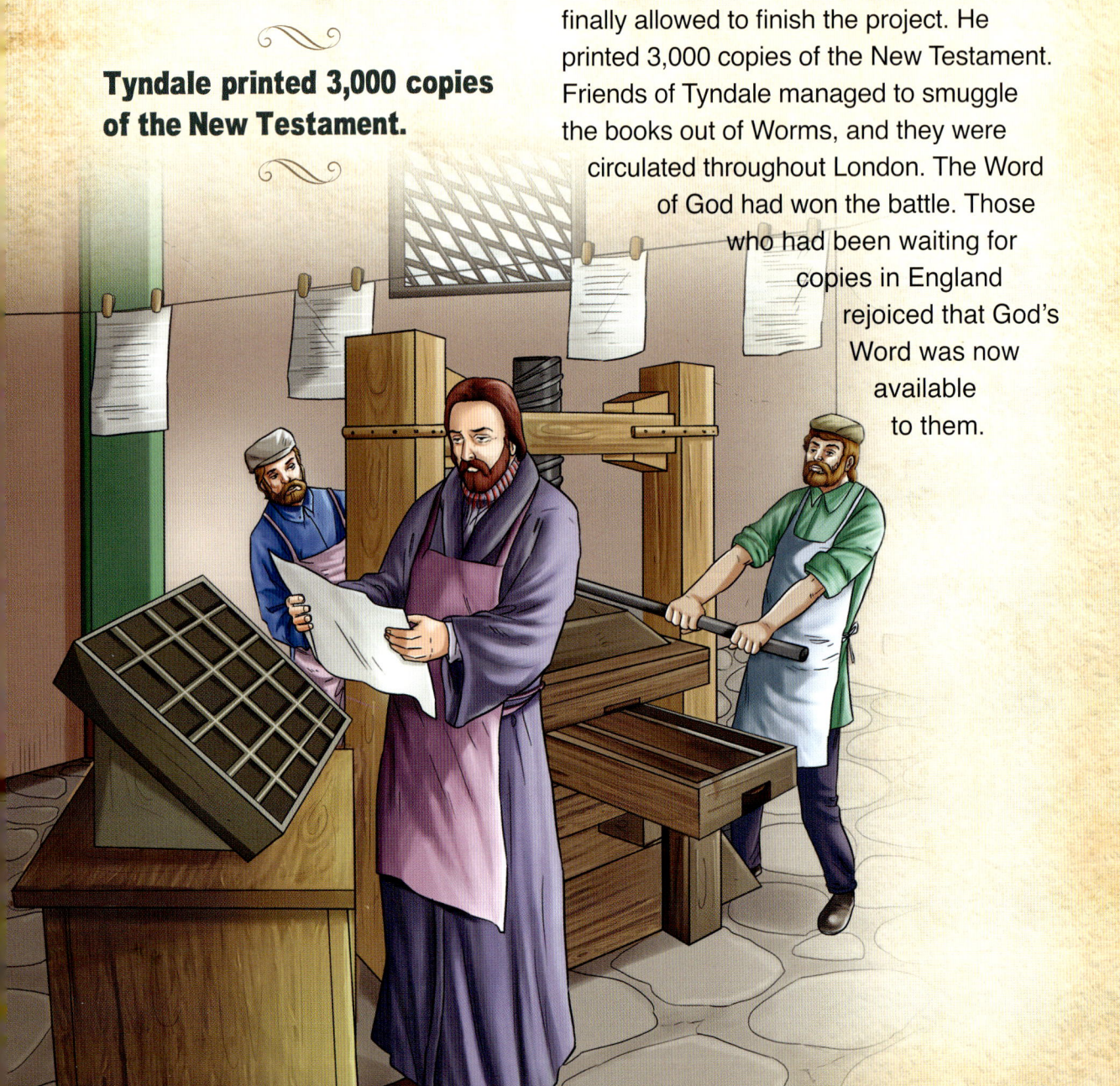

The Church of Rome tried everything they could to destroy Tyndale's Bible. The bishop of Durham at one time bought all the copies of Tyndale's Bible in a bookstore and then burned them. He thought he was doing Tyndale great harm, but he actually did just the opposite. The money given for the Bibles was used to buy more materials for a new and better edition. In fact, without this money Tyndale's new project would not have been possible.

Unfortunately, on one of his trips to smuggle Bibles into England on a merchant ship, Tyndale was betrayed into the hands of his enemies. Because of his work in translating the Scriptures, they threw him into prison, where he suffered for many months.

Church leaders came to him in prison to make a deal with him. They offered him his freedom if he would tell them the names of those who had helped pay to print the first edition of his Bible. Tyndale freely admitted that the bishop of Durham had helped him the most by buying up large numbers of his Bibles.

When the church finally gave him a trial months later, it was a ridiculous charade. Tyndale was tried and convicted for heresy. It is hard to believe that the church, which was started by Jesus to spread the gospel, wanted to execute Tyndale because he was making copies of God's Word!

Unfortunately, King Henry VIII, a Christian himself, did nothing to help Tyndale. He was afraid of the church leaders and allowed them to go through with their wicked plan. Satan was behind all of this, of course. He didn't want the light of the gospel to come to England, and hoped its people would remain forever in spiritual darkness.

So Tyndale was sentenced to be burned at the stake in the prison yard. But he was brave. Before he died, his last words in prayer were, "Lord, open the eyes of the king of England." And God did just that. The reformer's prayer was answered three years later in 1539, when King Henry VIII eventually did see the light.

Today William Tyndale is considered the father of the English

Reformation and the apostle of England. He was a brilliant scholar who was used by God to profoundly change history. He bravely led the way so that other reformers could follow. Fortunately, Thomas Cromwell and Thomas More continued Tyndale's work after his death. Others, such as John and Charles Wesley in the 1700s, also helped bring the gospel to the common people of England.

Before Tyndale died, his last words in prayer were, "Lord, open the eyes of the king of England."

God has always had His champions to shed the light of the gospel on the pathway to heaven. Time and again, when the way has seemed the darkest, the light of truth has broken forth to bring the dawn.

Today, we must also stand up for God. We can do great things for Jesus when we use the Bible to tell the gospel story, just as Tyndale did. We can give a Bible to someone who doesn't have one. Or we might be able to help pay for the translation of the Bible in a language that has not yet been finished.

Today, Bible societies all over the world are working together to translate the Bible. The goal of these Bible societies is to make sure that the Bible is printed in every language and dialect on earth. When that happens, the gospel will go to all the world. "And this gospel of the kingdom will be preached in all the world as a witness to all the nations, and then the end will come" (Matthew 24:14).

Our Prayer:

"Dear Father in heaven, thank You for keeping the Bible safe all these years. Thank You for brave people such as William Tyndale, who were not afraid to risk their life so that the Bible could be read by everyone."

Hidden Treasure Questions:

- ✓ Why did William Tyndale want the common people to have a Bible in their own language?
- ✓ Who was the king of England at that time?

Listen to this story online!

Scan for bonus content

John Bunyan Jailed

This story is taken from *The Great Controversy*, chapter 14.

During the 1600s, the Church of Rome fought back against the Protestant reformers who tried to spread the gospel. More and more Protestant pastors were being thrown out of their churches because they preached the gospel of Jesus.

John Bunyan was one of those English pastors who stood bravely for Jesus. He was a very popular speaker, because he preached from the heart and was a wonderful storyteller. He was so interesting that many of the common people began leaving the other congregations in Bedford, England, to come and hear him preach at his church.

In his church in Bedford, John criticized the government-run church, telling everyone that church leaders had no right to tell people what to believe and how and when they should worship. He went on to tell them that only God's grace could save them.

John was not liked by the priests in the Church of England. Eventually they convinced the local magistrate that he was breaking the law and needed to be jailed.

So during one of his weekly sermons, the constable came right into John's church and arrested him. The Bedford jail became his home, where he spent a great deal of time during the next 12 years. Many criminals were in that jail, and at first it was hard for John. Then he decided to make the best use of his time by preaching to the men, sometimes 40 or 50 at a time. With John in the jail cell, it seemed that heaven was very near, and soon many were giving their hearts to Jesus.

John would stay in jail for three or four months at a time. But he was such a friendly person that everyone loved him, and eventually the jailer would just send him home. The priests and magistrate would try to keep him there, but the jailer sympathized with John. "How can a man like Mr. Bunyan be trouble for the law?" he would always say.

The magistrate would tell John that he could stay out of jail if he would only stop his preaching. But John would not do this. Sooner or later they would come looking for him and send him back to jail again.

On one occasion when John had been sent home, a local priest happened to walk by his home and saw him through an open window with his family. He knew that John was supposed to be in jail, so he sent word to the magistrate that he might want to check the jail to see if John was actually there.

Meanwhile, John was at home eating the evening meal with his family. However, he was impressed that he should go back to the jail for the evening. So when supper was over, he headed back to the Bedford jail and locked himself in his cell as he always did, without even bothering to tell the jailer.

About an hour later the magistrate showed up with the priest to make an inspection as the priest had asked. "Good evening, warden!" they said cheerfully. "Are all your prisoners doing well?"

"Yes," the warden said, wondering what they might be up to.

"Is John Bunyan here as well?"

> **During one of his weekly sermons, the constable came right into John's church and arrested him.**

"Yes, he is," the jailer replied, knowing that it wasn't true and that he was probably going to get into trouble because of his habit of letting John out.

"Well, let's see him then," the magistrate ordered.

The jailer got his keys and walked the two men to John's cell. There to his surprise he found the prisoner reading a book by candlelight.

The priest was surprised, and the magistrate was not at all happy with the priest.

After the two visitors left, the jailer stopped by John's cell again. "That was a close call," he sighed with relief. "I was shocked to find you in your cell! I thought that you were home with your family!"

"I was," John said with a twinkle in his eye, "but for some reason I felt impressed by the Holy Spirit that I should come back tonight."

The jailer could only shake his head in wonder. "I'm not going to tell you when you can go home anymore, John, or when you should come back to jail. If God speaks to you like that, I am sure that the two of you can manage it much better than I."

John went on to write *Pilgrim's Progress* while in jail. The book was published in 1678 and is still a very famous book. It has now been published in more than 200 languages.

Today, John Bunyan's story still wins people to Jesus. No sacrifice was too great for him. His years in prison were a small price to pay for God's promise of eternal life.

When supper was over, John headed back to the Bedford jail and locked himself in his cell as he always did.

Our Prayer:

"Dear Father, help me to be cheerful, even when times are hard. It may be that I can win someone to Jesus by my example."

Hidden Treasure Questions:

✓ Why did everyone like to hear John Bunyan preach?

✓ Why did the jailer let John leave the jail from time to time?

Listen to this story online!

Scan for bonus content

Christians Flee to America

This story is taken from *The Great Controversy*, chapter 16.

By the early 1600s, there were many countries in Europe that wanted to be free from the power of the Church of Rome. They didn't believe that church leaders were following the Bible teachings as they should, and they didn't believe that the church should be telling them what they could and could not do.

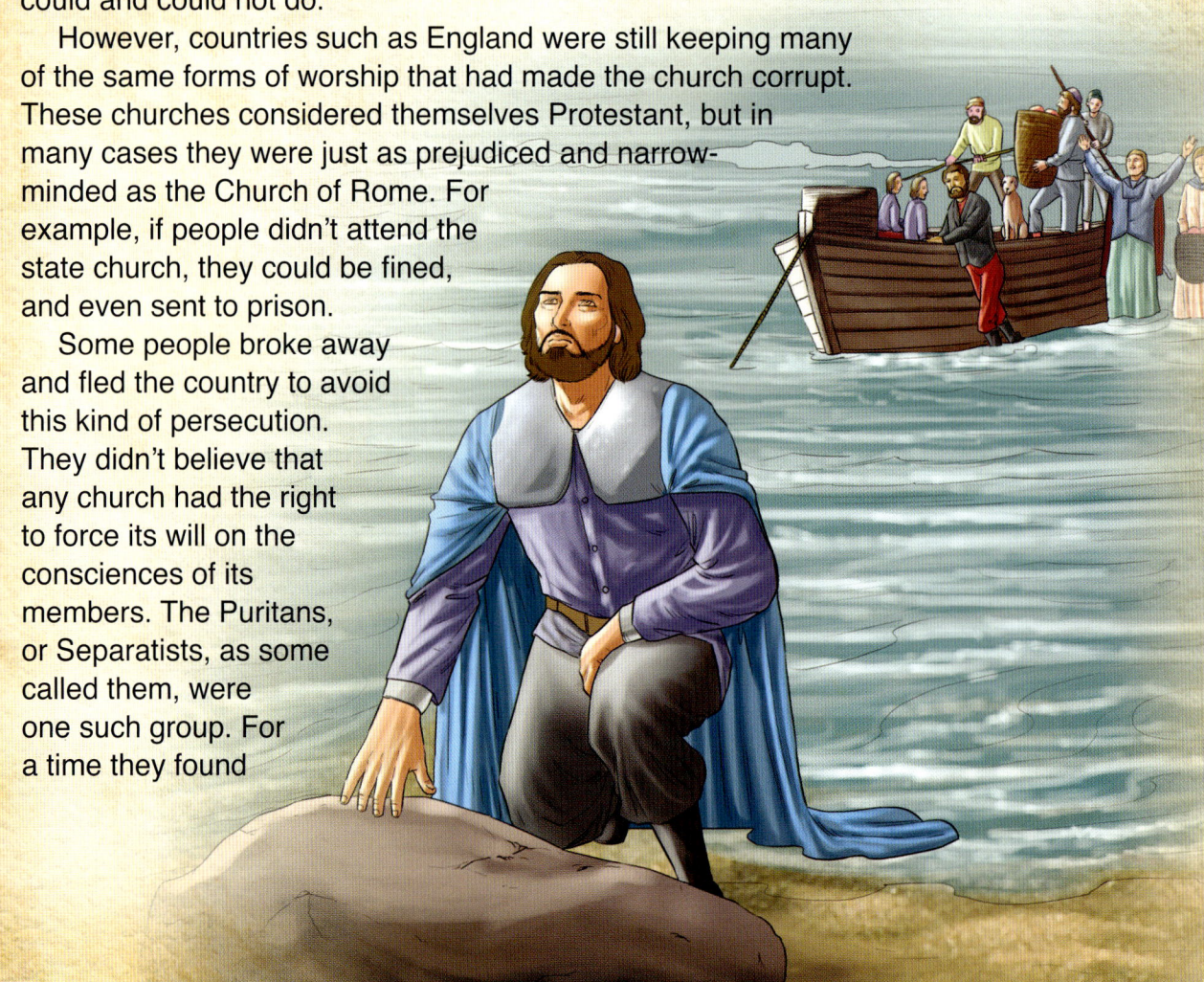

However, countries such as England were still keeping many of the same forms of worship that had made the church corrupt. These churches considered themselves Protestant, but in many cases they were just as prejudiced and narrow-minded as the Church of Rome. For example, if people didn't attend the state church, they could be fined, and even sent to prison.

Some people broke away and fled the country to avoid this kind of persecution. They didn't believe that any church had the right to force its will on the consciences of its members. The Puritans, or Separatists, as some called them, were one such group. For a time they found a safe refuge in countries such as Holland, later known as the Netherlands.

It was a hard life for them. The Puritans wanted a pure form of religion without all the fancy ceremonies and proud fanfare. But to get it they had to leave their homes and businesses behind. It didn't seem as if things would be changing back in England any time soon. During these times, their love and devotion to God had grown strong. They could see that God's angels were with them to protect them, and that He was providing for their every need.

A group of Puritans finally decided that they must leave Europe altogether. They had heard that the New World might be a good place to start over, and their pastor, John Robinson, encouraged them to take the step of faith. It was their hope that the new land would offer them a place where they could be free from persecution and be able to worship God as they saw best.

So they made plans to hire a ship to take them on the journey across the sea. Of course, they didn't know about the hardships that awaited them on the ocean or the dangers that they would find on the shores of America. Nor could they have known that they would be helping to begin a new nation that would stand for liberty and freedom of conscience.

A group of Puritans finally decided that they must leave Europe. They had heard that the New World might be a good place to start over.

Pastor Robinson could not go with them, but on his last day with them, he challenged them to be true to God. "Remember your covenant with God," he said. "Remember your promise to one another to receive whatever light and truth you find in the Word of God."

This group of honest, God-fearing people later became known as Pilgrims, and what a story they could tell us if we could talk to them today. The first ship that they chartered could not be used because of needed repairs. So they arranged for passage on another ship called the *Mayflower*.

By the time they had finally left England, it was late in the season. The North Atlantic was stormy during the autumn months, and the trip was dangerous. Food was bad, quarters were cramped below deck, and many people got sick on the voyage. There were 102 passengers who made the trip, and by the time they arrived on November 21, the winter weather had set in.

There were no warm homes awaiting them, and no stores where they could buy food. Rude huts were built for those who decided to live on shore, but many stayed on the ship until spring.

Of the 102 people who came to the new world on the *Mayflower*, 44 died due to disease, sickness, and exposure to the cold climate. If it hadn't been for the kindness of the Native American people who lived in the area, the colony would probably not have survived to establish itself.

Squanto, who had actually been a captive of an English exploration party earlier, became the Pilgrims' best friend. He had been taken captive to England, and then later made his way back to North America. He helped the Pilgrims find food in the forests and fields of Massachusetts, and then taught them how to plant corn in the weak New England soil.

The place where the Pilgrims settled was named Plymouth. The most famous of their leaders were John Alden, Myles Standish, and their governor, William Bradford. It was these Pilgrim fathers who helped establish the first permanent settlement in North America.

Unfortunately, the colony that developed from the Puritan group of believers eventually became very intolerant of people who did not believe as they did. This was a sad thing. They should have realized that the desire for religious freedom was the real reason they had all left England in the first place.

> **By the time they had finally left England, it was late in the season. The North Atlantic was stormy during the autumn months.**

Our Prayer:

"Dear Father, help me to be as faithful and loyal to You as the Pilgrims were."

Hidden Treasure Questions:

- ✓ What religious group did the Pilgrims belong to?
- ✓ Who helped the Pilgrim settlers survive in Massachusetts that first year?

Listen to this story online!

Scan for bonus content

Roger Williams

This story is taken from The Great Controversy, *chapter 16.*

Roger Williams was one of the most famous champions of religious freedom in the history of America. He was the first person in the modern Christian church to establish a government that would allow people the freedom to worship God as they pleased.

He was an honest seeker of truth. As the early Pilgrims had done, he came to enjoy religious freedom. He believed that this was the personal right of everyone, whatever their religion. "We can try to control crime," he said. "But we should never try to control the conscience."

This idea had not been accepted in England for years, and that was why so many were coming to the New World. Not going to church was not an option in the European churches, and even in the churches in the Massachusetts Bay Colony it was required. People who failed to attend were fined and often put in prison.

Roger Williams thought this was ridiculous. "Why would we want to force people to worship who are unwilling and not religious?" he said.

He was respected and loved as a pastor. He was kind, generous, and open-minded, and wherever he went the common people accepted him lovingly.

However, he also insisted that government leaders should not make the rules for churches. He believed that government should run the country, and the church should run the church. That was what finally got him into trouble. Government leaders in the Massachusetts Bay Colony banished him, and to avoid arrest, he had to flee to the wild forests of New England during the cold winter.

He wandered in the wilderness for 14 weeks, not knowing if he would survive. "But the ravens fed me," he said. Sometimes his shelter at night was a hollow tree. Finally, he found a home among the Native Americans who lived in the area.

Roger Williams is most famous for the colony that he established on land given to him by the Narragansett tribe of Native Americans. He shared the gospel story with the Narragansett tribe and eventually wrote a dictionary of the Narragansett language to help people communicate with the tribe.

This settlement eventually became the colony and state of Rhode Island. It was where complete religious freedom was given to Colonists for the first time in the Americas. The main principle of the government there was "that every man should have liberty to worship God according to the light of his own conscience."

His colony became the home for thousands who had been persecuted religiously in Europe, and even in other colonies of America. Eventually, the freedoms this colony represented became the cornerstone of the United States of America.

The Declaration of Independence in America would later state clearly: "We hold these truths to be self-evident, that all men are created equal, that they are endowed by their Creator with certain unalienable rights, that among these, are life, liberty, and the pursuit of happiness. This means that we are all equal in God's

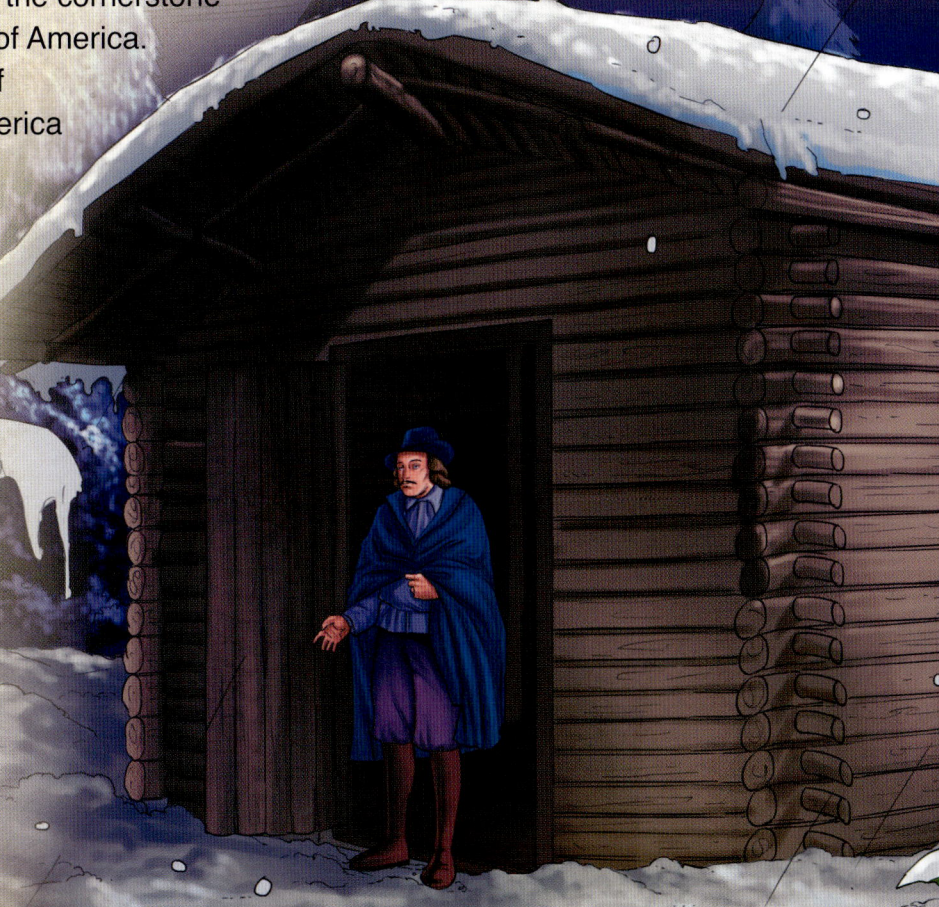

> **Eventually, the freedoms this colony represented became the cornerstone of the United States of America.**

eyes, and that we should treat one another as though we believe that. Our rights are given to us by God, and no one should be able to take them away from us.

Roger Williams shared the gospel story with the Narragansett tribe.

The Constitution of the United States of America adds wisdom to these ideas when it says, "Congress shall make no law respecting an establishment of religion, or prohibiting the free exercise thereof." In other words, no government should be able to make a law that will give special privileges to certain churches or religions. And no one should have so much power that they can make other people worship the way they want them to worship. We should respect everyone's right to worship as they think is best.

This does not mean that worshipping however you want will please God. When we worship God, we need to follow His plan. The Bible tells us what God's plan is, and we need to follow that plan very carefully. If we don't, we will let our own wants change the way we worship. The Bible tells us what will happen if we do that. "There is a way that seems right to a man, but its end is the way of death" (Proverbs 14:12).

Our Prayer:

"Dear God, thank You so much for the religious freedoms that You have given us today. One day, they will be taken away from us, and we pray that You will help us to be strong for You when it happens."

Hidden Treasure Questions:

- ✓ What was the name of the man who started the colony of Rhode Island?
- ✓ What kinds of people were welcome in Roger Williams' colony?

Listen to this story online!

Scan for bonus content

Saved From a Fire

This story is taken from *The Great Controversy*, chapter 14.

God has had men and women in every generation who were not afraid to stand up against wrong and speak for Him. John Wesley and his younger brother, Charles, were that kind of people. They were known for their humbleness, kindness in helping others, and godly prayer life. They were destined to have many hardships in their lives, but because of their missionary spirit, they were able to do great things for God. God blessed them, and eventually they became some of the best-known religious reformers of their time.

The boys were born in the early 1700s to a family with 19 children. Their mother and father believed that education was very important and taught the children to read as soon as they could walk and talk. The parents were very strict and insisted that their children all learn to read and write both Greek and Latin. Every day before lunch and every night before bed, John's mother would ask questions of each child about what they had studied that day.

While just a boy of 5, John almost died in a fire that burned their house down. The parents managed to get all of the children out of the house except John. However, just before the roof collapsed, a church member standing on a neighbor's shoulders lifted him out through a second-story window. This amazing rescue made John later feel that God had saved him for a special purpose in life.

As young men, John and Charles were ordained to be ministers. One of their first assignments was to go to America as missionaries in the Georgia Colony.

On board the ship to America, they were impressed with a group of German Moravians. Then suddenly a storm came up. The sea was so violent that it washed up over the deck, split the mainsail in pieces, and poured down into the ship's hold.

> **John almost died in a fire. Just before the roof collapsed, a church member standing on a neighbor's shoulders lifted him out through a second-story window.**

Everyone on board was terribly frightened. Most screamed out in terror, but not the Moravians. They were calm and had the peace of heaven on their faces. None of them looked as if they were afraid to die, not even the children.

In America, the Wesley brothers stayed with the Moravians for a while in Savannah, Georgia. They noticed that they were a simple people. Their worship style was solemn and yet deeply spiritual. Their services were nothing like the cold, lifeless services held in the formal Church of England back home.

On the return trip to England, a Moravian preacher helped John understand the great truths of the Bible better. He helped him see that there is nothing anyone can do to save himself and that only through Jesus can we receive salvation. This was a wonderful discovery for John, who had been raised to believe that the more good things one did, the more holy he became. When John realized that all he needed to do was pray and then Jesus would forgive him of every sin, his life was changed forever.

John's heart burned with a desire to spread the good news of what he had learned. God's grace was free! Everywhere he went, he preached the simple story of Jesus' love and His great sacrifice on the cross. Thousands soon learned that John preached such as no one else in England. Hundreds of people would pack the churches where he came to speak.

Other preachers caught the fire of John's message and began to preach this message in their churches, too. Few of them agreed on every doctrine taught in the Bible, but the Spirit of God inspired them to lead others to Jesus.

John and Charles formed a "holy club" because they believed that living pure lives was the most important thing to God. They met every morning from 6:00 to 9:00 for prayer and Bible reading. On Wednesdays and Fridays, they fasted until 3:00 in the afternoon. Because of their unusual methods of study and simple living, some began calling them "Methodists." Eventually, their church organization became known by that name.

The two brothers had no wish to start a new church group. They just wanted people to serve God and worship Him as the Bible told them they should. They didn't think that the strict, formal ceremonies of the official Church of England were a blessing to people. During the Protestant Reformation in Europe, God had set the people of England free from the chains of spiritual darkness laid on them by the Church of Rome. Unfortunately, the churches had almost lost sight of what Martin Luther and the other reformers had taught just two centuries before.

But this was all about to change. God was leading a religious revival in England, and the Wesley brothers were going to be a big part of it.

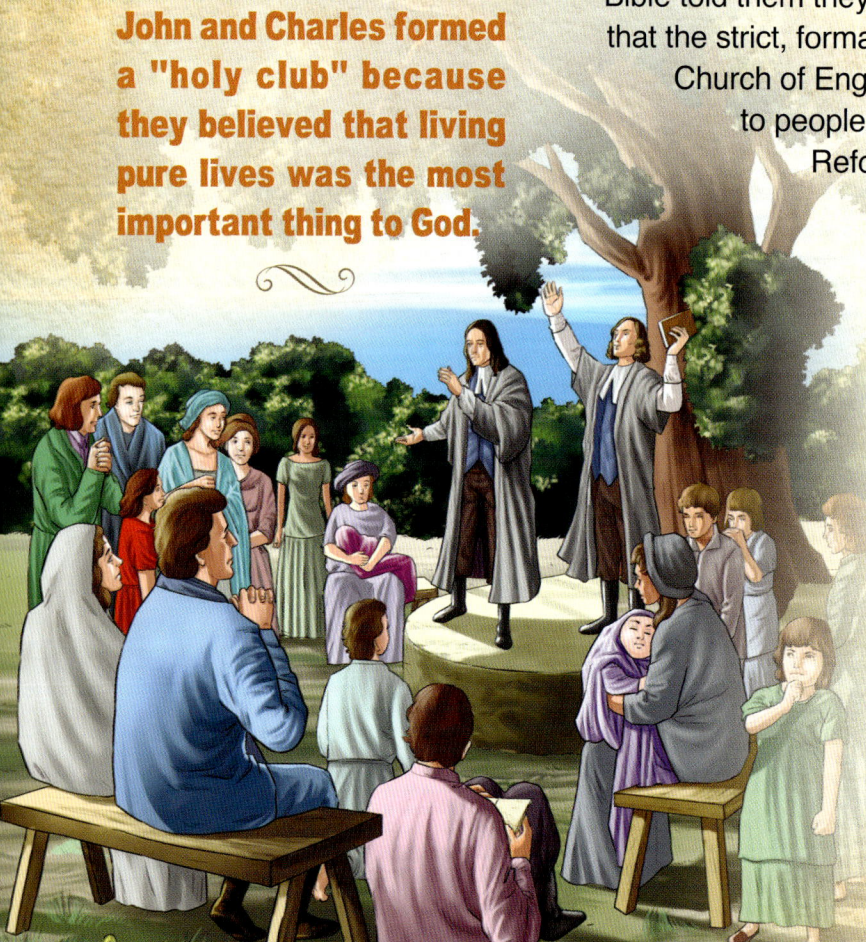

> **John and Charles formed a "holy club" because they believed that living pure lives was the most important thing to God.**

Our Prayer:

"Dear Jesus, help me to love You and serve You as faithfully as John and Charles Wesley did."

Hidden Treasure Questions:

✓ How old was John when he almost died in a fire?

✓ What was the name of the German religious group that John traveled with on a ship to America?

Listen to this story online!

Scan for bonus content

Two Brothers Dedicated to God

This story is taken from *The Great Controversy*, chapter 14.

John and Charles Wesley became famous for the godly lives that they lived and the simple gospel that they preached. However, they could see that the Church of England was very corrupt, and they began to preach that changes were needed in the church. Of course, the church leaders were not happy about this, and before long they were persecuting the two brothers.

Then many rich and powerful preachers in London decided not to let them preach in their churches anymore. But that didn't stop John and Charles. They decided that if they couldn't preach indoors, then they would preach outdoors.

And so, more and more, the two brothers began to preach in meetings that were held outdoors. This was hard for John and his brother, because they had always been taught that preaching should be done only inside churches. However, soon thousands came to hear them preach. There were many people who were not allowed in the Church of England. They were considered too sinful to be allowed in church. Now they could hear the message that God gave to John and Charles. God is so amazing! He always has a plan to include everybody.

But the local ministers would not leave them alone. John became a very popular preacher, and as his fame spread, so did the jealousy of the local preachers.

Soon these preachers were stirring up the people in towns along the way where John traveled. Often he had to flee for his life when ugly rumors were spread about him. Many times he escaped death only because God sent His angels to protect him on his missions of mercy to preach the Word of God.

One day, John was traveling through an English village when he was met by an angry mob. Satan had stirred these men up, and they wanted to kill him. John asked what he had done to deserve this, but the crowd kept shouting, "Kill him! Kill him!"

When John prayed for the mob, several leaders of the riot suddenly turned on the crowd as if the Holy Spirit was speaking to them. "Leave him alone!" they shouted.

Then, making a tight circle around John, they said, "We will defend you with our lives! Follow us, and not one soul will touch a hair on your head!"

Several others now joined John's protectors and tried to pull the mob away from him. But the number of people in the angry mob kept growing, and many clambered to get near enough to hurt him. The crowd began pushing John along a slippery path down a hill. Some tried to throw him to the ground, but they couldn't get a good hold of his coat.

A big man behind John tried to hit him on the head. However, every time the man tried to hit him, the blows were turned aside miraculously.

A big man behind John tried to hit him on the head with an oak stick. John couldn't move one way or the other, and one blow from the stick would have been enough to knock him out. However, every time the man tried to hit him, the blows were turned aside miraculously.

Another time, a wild mob was chasing John and began throwing things at him. A stone hit him between the eyes, but he felt as if only a blade of grass had hit him. Someone punched him in the face, and though the blood gushed from his mouth, he never felt any pain.

John was a humble man who tried to live unselfishly, just as Jesus had done. When he had money, he usually gave most of it away to those in need. Because of his fame in England, he eventually became quite wealthy. One year he made about 1,400 pounds, but managed to live on a mere 30 pounds (about $72). The rest he gave away to the poor, the hungry, and the sick.

One of his famous quotes shows how he felt about giving. "Do all the good you can, by all the means you can, in all the ways you can, in all the places you can, at all the times you can, to all the people you can, as long as ever you can."

For more than a half century, John and Charles Wesley served God faithfully. It is estimated that their work in England brought more than a half-million people to Jesus.

Charles became a famous songwriter, and we still sing some of his hymns in church today. John is best known for his writings and theology that helped him and his brother start a religious revolution in England. Truly these were men of God.

> **Making a tight circle around John, they said, "We will defend you with our lives!"**

Our Prayer:

"Dear Father in heaven, thank You for the protection that angels give us every day, just as they did for John and Charles Wesley."

Hidden Treasure Questions:

- ✓ Who usually stirred up the mobs to hurt John Wesley?

- ✓ How many people were brought to Jesus because of the work of John and Charles Wesley?

Listen to this story online!

Scan for bonus content

God Is Banned in France

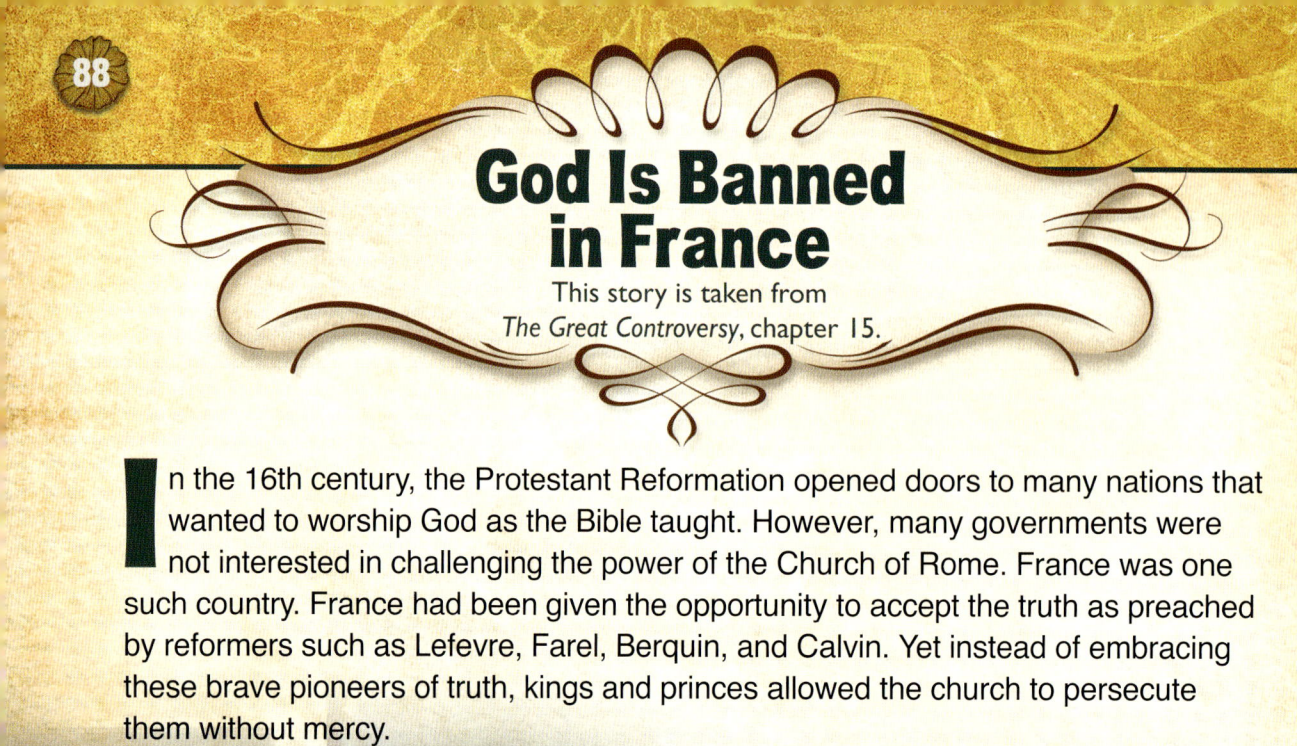

This story is taken from
The Great Controversy, chapter 15.

In the 16th century, the Protestant Reformation opened doors to many nations that wanted to worship God as the Bible taught. However, many governments were not interested in challenging the power of the Church of Rome. France was one such country. France had been given the opportunity to accept the truth as preached by reformers such as Lefevre, Farel, Berquin, and Calvin. Yet instead of embracing these brave pioneers of truth, kings and princes allowed the church to persecute them without mercy.

Now France was paying for it. Because of the persecution, tens of thousands of Christians had been martyred, and hundreds of thousands more fled the country. With these exiles went the skilled people of the country, all the good moral people, and most of the educated people. Those who were left were bigoted, superstitious, and violent. Their goal now was to get rid of religion once and for all. Although the church leaders did not clearly see what the results would be, they should have. Had not Jesus Himself said, "All who take the sword will perish by the sword" (Matthew 26:52)?

The problems all seemed to come to a head in 1789. France had been at war for many years and had begun to tax the people heavily. Poor people resented the rich and those in power. The king and his courtiers lived extravagantly in their palaces, but so did the bishops and cardinals of Rome.

The feudal system was still being used in France at that time, which meant that the rich people owned all the land. Poor, uneducated people had to work the land as farmers with little or no pay, and only sometimes with food being promised for their labor.

> **The king and his courtiers lived extravagantly in their palaces, but so did the bishops and cardinals of Rome.**

These leaders had been abusing their power for centuries, and now the people of France rebelled against them! Why should they bow the knee to anyone? They wanted nothing to do with the rulers or the church that represented government powers. Even worse, they rebelled against God, whom they saw as a tyrant, like the church leaders in power.

Changes were soon made as a new government was set up by the revolution. A legislature was put in place of the king. Heavy taxes were no longer to be collected, and land was taken away from the rich to be given to the poor farmers.

However, the changes were not all good. Church doors were closed, Christians were executed, and the Bible was burned. People stood in the streets defying God, daring Him to punish them for their curses against His name.

A convention was called at which the leaders of the revolution declared that France was now a country for atheists. They said, "God doesn't have a place in our government anymore." Now "reason" would be their god. In other words, common sense would replace the truths of the Bible. A woman was set up as the "Goddess of Reason," and the church bishop of Paris was brought in to tell everyone that the Bible was a book of fables.

The frenzy of the revolution continued to grow, and soon everyone was crying for the death of the king. Finally, in January of 1793, King Louis XV was executed at the guillotine nearly four years after the revolution started. His wife, Marie Antoinette, was executed a few months later.

This began a time in the history books called the Reign of Terror. Those who had been in power were the first to be executed. For centuries the church had used the stake to burn its heretics, and now the revolutionary leaders set up the guillotine. Mobs of angry people swarmed all over Paris in search of former government and church leaders. Then they dragged them off to die violent deaths at the places of execution. History tells us that more than 40,000 people died that way.

No one could trust anyone. Those who criticized the revolution paid for it with their life. Those who had ordered the death of the king were soon sent to the guillotine too.

Chaos was everywhere. People were starving to death as there was a lack of food in the city. Robbers and looters were everywhere. The country was bankrupt. With all the troubles in France, people who could leave fled the country.

King David's famous words tell the story of France during the revolution. "The fool has said in his heart, 'There is no God'" (Psalm 14:1). If there is one lesson that we can learn from this terrible time in history, it is this: Humans cannot stamp out the Word of God. In the end, God always wins the war between good and evil. The gospel of Jesus will prevail!

> **The frenzy of the revolution continued to grow, and soon everyone was crying for the death of the king.**

Our Prayer:

"Dear God, the times are coming when our country will suffer hard times as they did in France. Help me to be ready for that day."

Hidden Treasure Questions:

✓ What year did the French Revolution begin?

✓ What replaced God and the Bible as the goddess of France?

Listen to this story online!

Scan for bonus content

Bloody Moon and Falling Stars

This story is taken from *The Great Controversy*, chapter 17, and based on Luke 21:25, 26; and Revelation 6:12, 13.

It is time for Jesus to come. God has given signs all around us telling us that it will happen, and that it will happen soon. Jesus said that before He comes again, things will happen that definitely point to His coming and to the end of the world.

Some of those events include fearful and great signs in the sky. Following the end of the medieval persecution that lasted until the 1700s, several signs appeared in the skies above the earth. In 1780, on May 19, there was a dark day in America when the sun didn't shine for a whole day, and the moon that night looked as if it had turned a bloodred color. Then on November 13 in 1833, a fantastic shower of meteors danced across the skies off of the United States. Matthew 24 talks about those events. "Immediately after the tribulation of those days the sun will be darkened, and the moon will not give its light; the stars will fall from heaven" (Matthew 24:29).

Some people don't think that we should use these events as signs of Jesus' Second Coming because they did not happen everywhere in the world at the same time. But not many of the signs that Jesus gave would take place everywhere in the world. If they did, such as with wars, famines, or major earthquakes, there would not be many people left alive on earth.

There are many other signs of Jesus' soon coming, and they are all around us. Besides wars, famines, and earthquakes, the Bible warns us of major disease epidemics. Then there is the increase in technology and scientific discoveries. All of these things have been predicted in the Bible. They are all helping to fulfill the Bible prophecy that the coming of Jesus is right around the corner. Add to these the increase in religious

> **On November 13 in 1833, a fantastic shower of meteors danced across the skies off of the United States.**

power the world over and the fact that satanic cults are being sold to us in books, movies, and video games. Now you can see what the Bible is trying to tell us. Most important, the gospel is going to go to the whole world, and then Jesus will come.

Wars are a sign that Jesus will come soon (Matthew 24:6-8). During the last century, the world has seen more than 100 major wars, and 160 million people have died. During World War II, in the 1940s, there were more than 75 million people killed, and in one decade alone China killed more than 70 million people. The continent of Africa has had many wars in modern history, and the worldwide war on terror right now is pretty scary all by itself.

What about famines? They are definitely a sign of Jesus' coming (Matthew 24:7). Experts tell us that in the past 100 years the world has seen 30 major famines, and more than 70 million people have died from starvation. Some of these famines are caused by droughts because of very little rain, and some are a result of wars. As the time draws nearer for Jesus to come again, it is not likely that famines will decrease because the world's population is growing very fast.

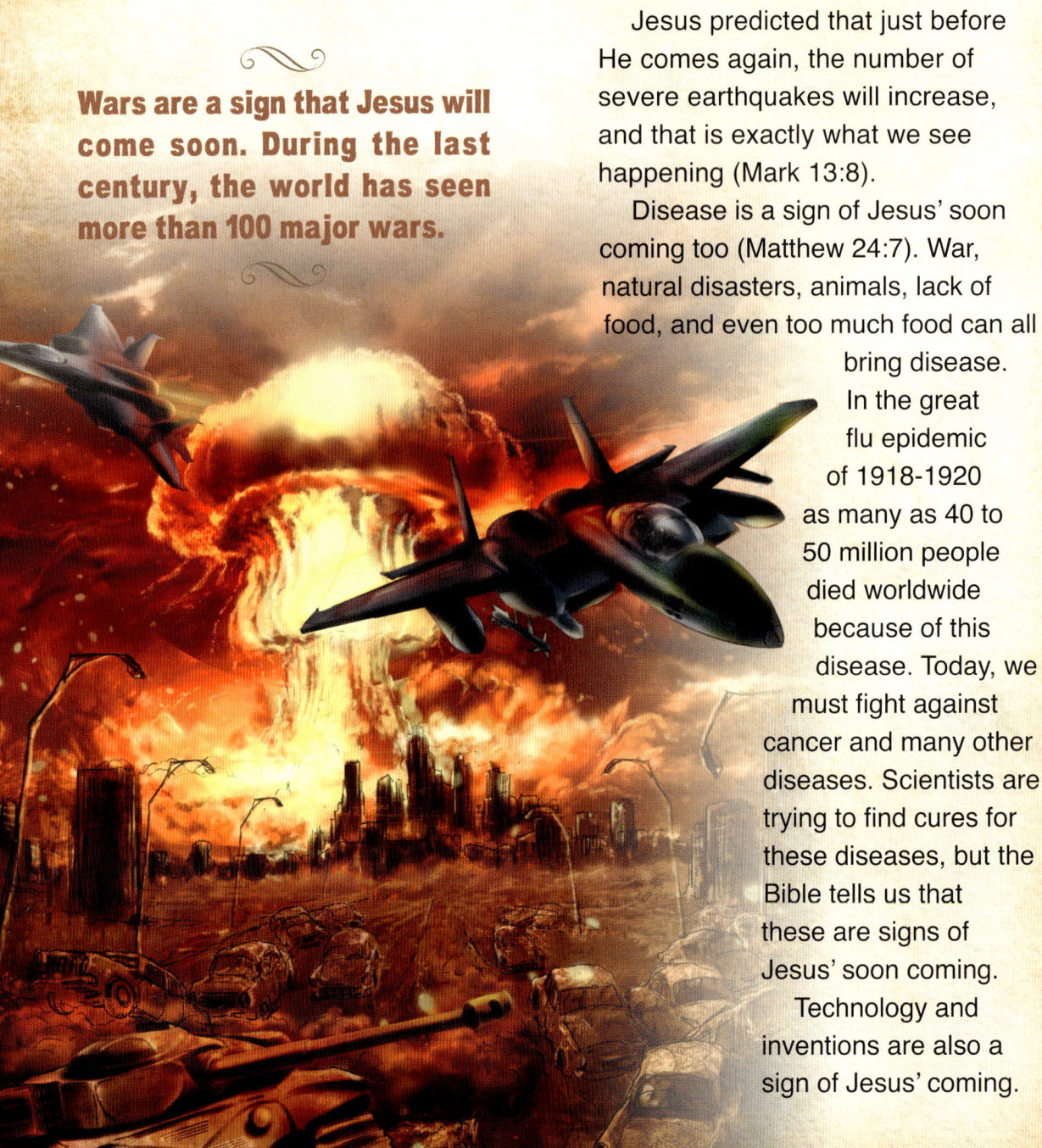

Wars are a sign that Jesus will come soon. During the last century, the world has seen more than 100 major wars.

Jesus predicted that just before He comes again, the number of severe earthquakes will increase, and that is exactly what we see happening (Mark 13:8).

Disease is a sign of Jesus' soon coming too (Matthew 24:7). War, natural disasters, animals, lack of food, and even too much food can all bring disease. In the great flu epidemic of 1918-1920 as many as 40 to 50 million people died worldwide because of this disease. Today, we must fight against cancer and many other diseases. Scientists are trying to find cures for these diseases, but the Bible tells us that these are signs of Jesus' soon coming. Technology and inventions are also a sign of Jesus' coming.

Daniel talks about a time in world history when knowledge will be increased (Daniel 12:4). Well, that time is certainly now. We are communicating with each other almost nonstop through cell phones, iPads, and the Internet. We fly fighter jets at astounding speeds, and they are capable of mass destruction. Our trains can go faster than 200 miles per hour, and spaceships fly to the moon.

We have communication satellites, cars that start by remote voice control, smart refrigerators, computers on our steering wheels, and GPS devices in our cell phones. Open heart surgeries that were almost impossible not many years ago are all but routine now. These are all signs of Jesus' soon coming.

Religious powers fighting in the world are a sign of Jesus' soon coming (Matthew 24:5-10, Revelation 12:17). Christians, Muslims, Jews, and Buddhists are all fighting one another more now than in recent history.

One of the scariest signs of Jesus' coming is the growing power that Satan has over the minds of people. Today, the occult is everywhere to deceive the world, and especially young people. We see it in books, movies, video games, exercise clubs, and even our churches. It is happening just as Peter said it would, because our enemy the devil prowls around like a roaring lion looking for someone to devour (1 Peter 5:8).

One of the most important signs of Jesus' coming is the fact that the gospel is going to all the world (Matthew 24:14). The Bible has been printed in more than 530 languages. Television, radio, satellite, and the Internet are spreading the good news faster every day. And when the whole world has heard the gospel story of salvation in Jesus, He will come. Jesus promised it would happen.

We cannot deny the signs of the times. They are everywhere—wars, natural disasters, famines, disease, technology and inventions, religious powers fighting one another, and the occult. Most important, the gospel has now been preached almost everywhere in the whole world. All of these signs clearly point us to the end of the world and the coming of Jesus. The Bible tells us so, and whether we are ready or not, Jesus will come. Even people in the world who are not religious can see that something very big is going to happen soon. The signs all around us are so obvious.

One of the most important signs of Jesus' coming is the fact that the gospel is going to all the world.

It is time for God's people to help the angels. They wait impatiently for us to tell our friends and neighbors that Jesus is coming. We have the hope that Jesus will soon come. We know about all of this because of the Bible, and that means we should be willing to tell the good news to everyone we meet. "Now it is high time to awake out of sleep; for now our salvation is nearer than when we first believed" (Romans 13:11).

Our Prayer:

"Dear Father in heaven, it is so exciting to see the signs all around us pointing to the soon coming of Jesus. Please help me to study Your Word so that I will not miss any of those signs."

Hidden Treasure Questions:

- ✓ What signs have you noticed in the news lately that tell us that Jesus is coming soon?

- ✓ Do you know some Bible texts that tell about Jesus' soon coming? Why not make a list and start memorizing some of those verses today?

Listen to this story online!

Scan for bonus content

A Little Boy Makes a Big Decision

This story is taken from
The Great Controversy, chapter 20.

Following the capture of the pope in the late 1700s, real changes came in Europe and other countries in which Christianity could be found. The control that the church had over the people was now broken.

The gospel began to go to the world such as it hadn't done since the days of the early church that was started by Jesus and the disciples. It seemed that the energy of God's Spirit was inspiring people to take the gospel to the world. Bible societies began springing up. Missionary organizations began sending missionaries to foreign countries. It was the beginning of the Great Awakening, and with it came a new excitement for the work of the gospel.

Dr. Joseph Wolff was one very unusual man who became a part of the Great Awakening. His desire was to take the gospel message to the world and to tell them about the Second Coming of Jesus. This desire all started when he was just a boy.

His father was a Jewish rabbi, and Joseph often listened to conversations his father had with other faithful Hebrews. They would discuss the future of their people, the coming Messiah, and the chance to go back to Jerusalem someday.

One day when he was only 7 years old, he was bragging to an old Christian neighbor about how blessed Israel was going to be when the Messiah came.

The old man told him kindly that the Messiah had already come and that the Jews had crucified Him. "Go home and read Isaiah 53, and you will be convinced that Jesus Christ is the Son of God," he added.

> **The old man told him kindly that the Messiah had already come and that the Jews had crucified Him.**

That conversation made a big impression on Joseph's young mind, and he did as the old man asked. He read the chapter for himself, and when he asked his father to explain it to him, his father would not talk about it. However, this only made him want to know more.

Joseph was a brilliant young man who was especially good at the study of languages. While in school, he became a Christian and decided that he wanted to be a missionary. In 1821, when he was 26, he began a lifelong work of spreading the gospel to the world.

As he preached, he studied about Jesus' life on earth and saw that the prophecies said that Jesus would come a second time. After further study, he realized that Jesus might come in just a few years. Some argued that Jesus had said, "No one knows the day nor the hour of Jesus' coming," but Dr. Wolff reminded them of the story of Noah. No one knew when the flood would come either. However, there were enough signs for everyone to see that it was near. So it will be with the coming of Jesus, he told them.

Dr. Wolff traveled to many places to share the gospel, including Egypt, Jerusalem, Persia, England, Ethiopia, India, and the United States. By now, everyone was calling him "the missionary to the world."

In his travels to America, he spoke to packed auditoriums in New York, Philadelphia, Baltimore, and Washington, D.C. United States government leaders even came to Congress Hall on Sabbath to hear him preach.

In his travels for Jesus, he was starved, attacked by robbers, condemned to death three times, shot at, and sold as a slave. He was given 200 blows to his feet and then made to walk on them all day. He was forced to walk over the mountains in the dead of winter with almost no clothes on.

Dr. Wolff survived because God sent heaven's angels to protect him.

Dr. Wolff survived all of these trials, partly because he was smart and witty, and partly because he could speak 14 languages. Among them were Chaldean, Persian, Hebrew, Arabic, English, and German. Of course, this helped him travel everywhere spreading the gospel, and many times his skill in speaking the local language was the only thing that saved his life.

But mostly he survived because God sent heaven's angels to protect him. His one goal in life was to win people to Jesus, and for this, God kept him from harm and danger. "Jesus of Nazareth is the true Messiah," he told Jews and Arabs alike. "He was the Man of Sorrows the first time He came, but the second time He comes will be in the clouds of heaven with the trump of the Archangel."

When Jesus returns again, we will be able to meet Joseph Wolff, and he will tell us about all of his adventures for Jesus. That will truly be an exciting day!

Our Prayer:

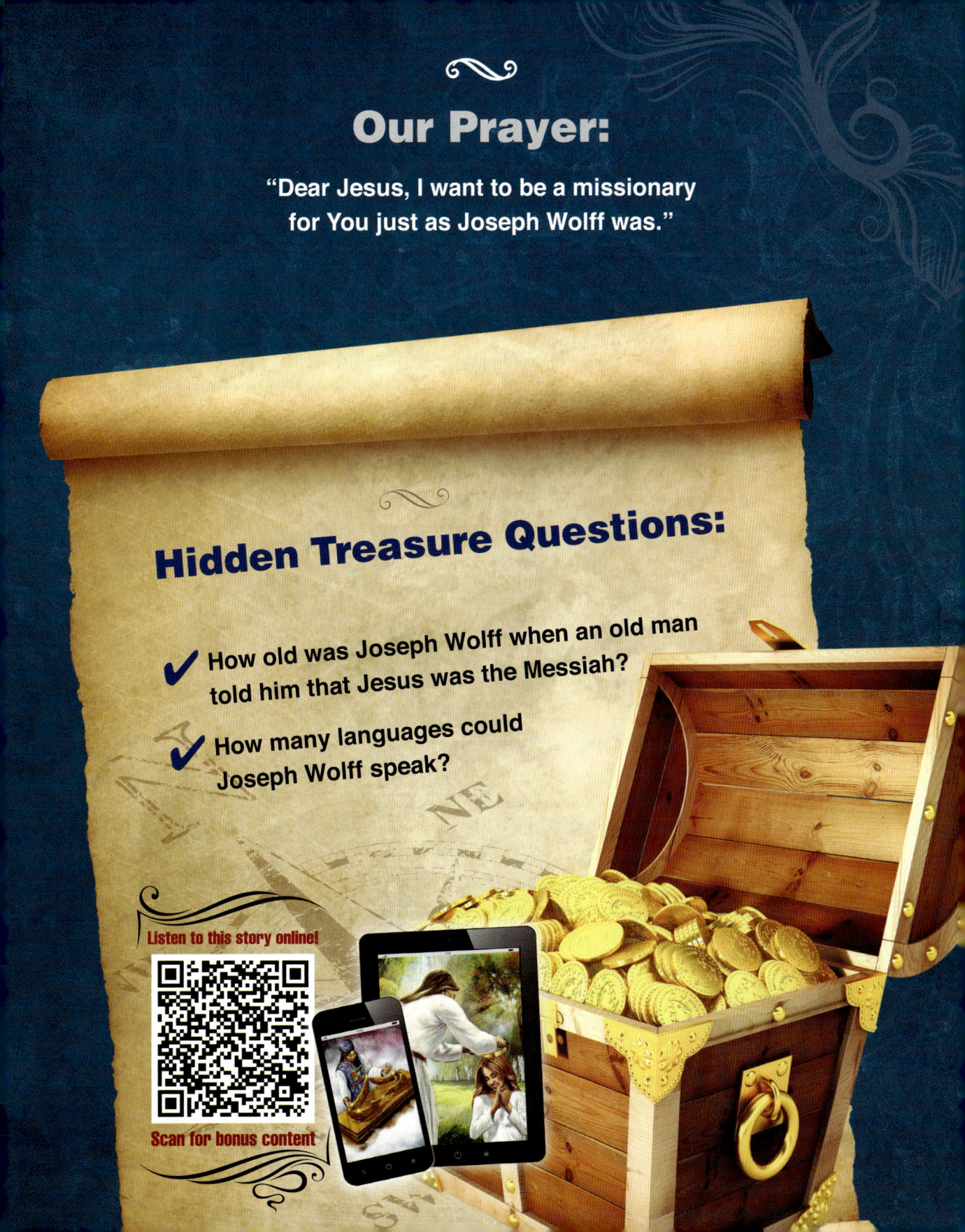

"Dear Jesus, I want to be a missionary for You just as Joseph Wolff was."

Hidden Treasure Questions:

✓ How old was Joseph Wolff when an old man told him that Jesus was the Messiah?

✓ How many languages could Joseph Wolff speak?

Listen to this story online!

Scan for bonus content

William Miller

This story is taken from The Great Controversy, chapter 18, and based on Daniel 8.

William Miller was a very special man destined to be the leader of a great revival in America. Little did he know that through the study of God's prophecies, he would help people see that Jesus was coming again, as the Bible prophecies had said He would.

Like many other reformers, William came from a poor family, but he learned to work hard and live a simple life. He was very smart, and although he liked to read and study a lot, he never did go to college.

While still a young man, he gave up his ideas of the God that we see in our Bibles and became a deist. A deist is someone who believes that God created the universe, but left us all to live and die on our own.

Later, he served in the military and fought against the British in the War of 1812. During the war, he had many close brushes with death. In one battle, he and the other American soldiers were vastly outnumbered by the British. Bombs, rockets, and shrapnel shells fell as thick as hailstones, and he feared for his life. One of these shells landed within two feet of him and exploded. It wounded three of his men and killed another, but Miller survived without a scratch. In the end, the American fighters somehow won the battle, and Miller was sure that God had helped them win.

After this experience, Miller no longer felt satisfied with his life as a deist. If there was no loving God of mercy, then death would be a scary thing to face. On the other hand, if there was a God and He was watching, Miller was going to have to answer for all the bad things he had done in his life.

When he returned home after the war, he started attending church again. The Holy Spirit impressed his young mind that there must be a loving, compassionate God who had given Himself to be the Savior of the world. If this was true, then the Bible had to be the Word of God.

Miller's friends made fun of him when they found out that he had become a Christian again, but he didn't care. He had found the greatest secret to happiness, and that was peace with God.

He began to study his Bible seriously, and found that God's Word tells us everything that we need to know about salvation. Verse by verse he went through the Bible, beginning with Genesis. When he came to the book of Daniel, he was surprised to find that this book held many keys to the future. The symbols and time prophecies of the Bible came alive for him.

Then he discovered the 2,300-day prophecy and learned that something big was going to happen soon. Miller read in Daniel 8:14 that after 2,300 days, the sanctuary was going to be cleansed.

He wasn't sure what that meant, but he studied some more and found out that the 2,300 days in Bible prophecy actually stood for 2,300 years. When he did his calculations, he learned that the 2,300 years would end in 1844, which was just a few years away. He knew that the prophecy had to come true, because all of the events predicted along the line of the 2,300-day prophecy had already been fulfilled. The making of the decree for Jerusalem to be rebuilt, the death of Jesus, and God's rejection of the Jews when they stoned Stephen had all happened just as Daniel had predicted. The only date that remained was 1844.

But what would happen in that year was a mystery.

Later, he served in the military and fought against the British in the War of 1812.

No one knew. Then Miller read that the Old Testament sanctuary service had a ceremony in which God cleansed the sanctuary of all sin. Miller knew that when Jesus came the second time at the end of the world, God would cleanse the world with fire. Maybe this was what Daniel 8:14 was talking about.

> **Miller read that the Old Testament sanctuary service had a ceremony in which God cleansed the sanctuary of all sin.**

Miller was overwhelmed with this new idea! If it was true, then the world was in for a big shock, because no one was talking about it. That was in 1818, and Miller believed that the world had only 25 more years to get ready.

"But how could this be so?" he wondered. Surely if this was right, someone would be talking about it. So he checked his calculations and studied all the prophecies again for five more years. There was no doubt in his mind. The prophecies all pointed to the coming of Jesus, and he must help others see it. But how? He was just a simple farmer.

Finally, he realized that he could no longer keep quiet. If God would send him an invitation, he would preach the good news of Jesus' coming to the world.

Our Prayer:

"Dear Jesus, thank You for giving us all of these amazing prophecies in the Bible."

Hidden Treasure Questions:

- ✓ What did Miller discover about the end of the world?
- ✓ What year did Miller think that Jesus would come again?

Listen to this story online!

Scan for bonus content

God Chooses a Simple Farmer

This story is taken from
The Great Controversy, chapter 18.

For years, William Miller had studied the Bible to understand the plan of salvation. Now he had made the greatest discovery of his life. Jesus was coming again, and He would come in just a few short years. The world needed to hear this wonderful message, but Miller was only a farmer and felt too shy to do it himself. For several years, he resisted God's call to preach what he had discovered. But the impression kept ringing in his ears, and he had no peace.

Then one day while he was out in his orchard praying, he made a deal with God. If the Lord would send someone with an invitation for Miller to preach, then he would go. He went back to his house quite satisfied that he was safe from such an offer. However, he hadn't been in the house more than a few minutes when there was a knock on the door. A messenger boy from a neighboring community had arrived with an invitation. Miller was asked to speak to the people on the topic of Bible prophecy and Jesus' soon coming.

Miller was shocked, but he kept his part of the bargain. He went to speak as he had promised he would. That was just the beginning. Soon he was being asked to go to many places to preach his messages from the book of Daniel and now Revelation.

He spoke about Nebuchadnezzar's image in Daniel 2. He told them that the parts of the image represented kingdoms that would come and go in world history, and in the end, God would set up a heavenly kingdom that would never end.

Miller used this prophecy in Daniel to show that God knows the future and revealed it all in the Bible for our benefit. He preached about other Bible prophecies too, such as the beasts in Daniel and Revelation and the three angels' messages in Revelation.

His most important message was always about the Second Coming of Jesus. Before long, he was the most popular speaker in New England. In every town where he went, dozens were converted and sometimes even hundreds.

Miller was asked to speak to the people on the topic of Bible prophecy and Jesus' soon coming.

Then on November 13, 1833, a Bible prophecy was fulfilled with the "falling of the stars." The meteor shower was so bright that it lit up the night sky. People everywhere saw this as a sign that Jesus would come soon, and this helped Miller make his point even more.

A time of great awakening was sweeping over the East Coast of the United States, and people were responding to the message of Jesus' soon coming. Alcohol dealers gave up their businesses and turned their shops into meeting rooms. Taverns and saloons were closed. Atheists, backslidden Christians, and the worst of sinners came to church now. At almost every hour of the day, people could be found having prayer meetings in towns all up and down the coast.

Thousands were coming to hear Miller preach, and the Holy Spirit used him in a powerful way. He traveled far and wide, and when people saw him for the first time, they were often surprised. He didn't look like a distinguished speaker. However, his preaching was powerful, and his calls for repentance were solemn. Audiences were held spellbound by his lectures, and his message brought people to their knees.

"The judgment hour of God is upon us," Miller always said, as he preached the three angels' messages. "Worship God, and come out of the false churches. God is looking for His faithful followers, who keep His commandments and have the faith of Jesus."

The newspapers had their fun, as we would expect. Unfortunately, Miller was rarely mentioned in them, except when the writers wanted to make fun of him. But that didn't stop Miller.

As 1844 drew closer, people tried to get Miller to tell them the exact time when Jesus would come, but he always resisted the temptation. "No one knows the day nor the hour," he would say.

However, some tried to set dates for the time when Jesus would come anyway, such as in the spring of 1843, and then again in the spring of 1844. When Jesus failed to come at those times, people were very discouraged. They wondered, "Have we made mistakes in our calculations?"

Then in the summer of 1844, a new message traveled across the United States. Jesus had tarried for some unknown reason, just like the bridegroom in the story of the 10 maidens with oil lamps. But now the date of His coming was set for October 22, 1844.

As that day approached, tens of thousands waited for Jesus to come. Businesses closed their shops again, and farmers didn't bother to harvest their crops. Jesus was coming. The power of the Holy Spirit in William Miller's preaching had done its job.

Imagine that it is October 21, 1844, and you are one of the thousands of Christians who are completely convinced that Jesus is returning tomorrow. What would you be doing? Be sure to read the next story to see exactly what happened on October 22, 1844!

Thousands were coming to hear Miller preach, and the Holy Spirit used him in a powerful way. He traveled far and wide.

Our Prayer:

"Lord, forgive me for the things I've done that hurt people. Help me to make these things right."

Hidden Treasure Questions:

- ✓ What deal did William Miller make with God about preaching?
- ✓ What was the final date set for the coming of Jesus?

Listen to this story online!

Scan for bonus content

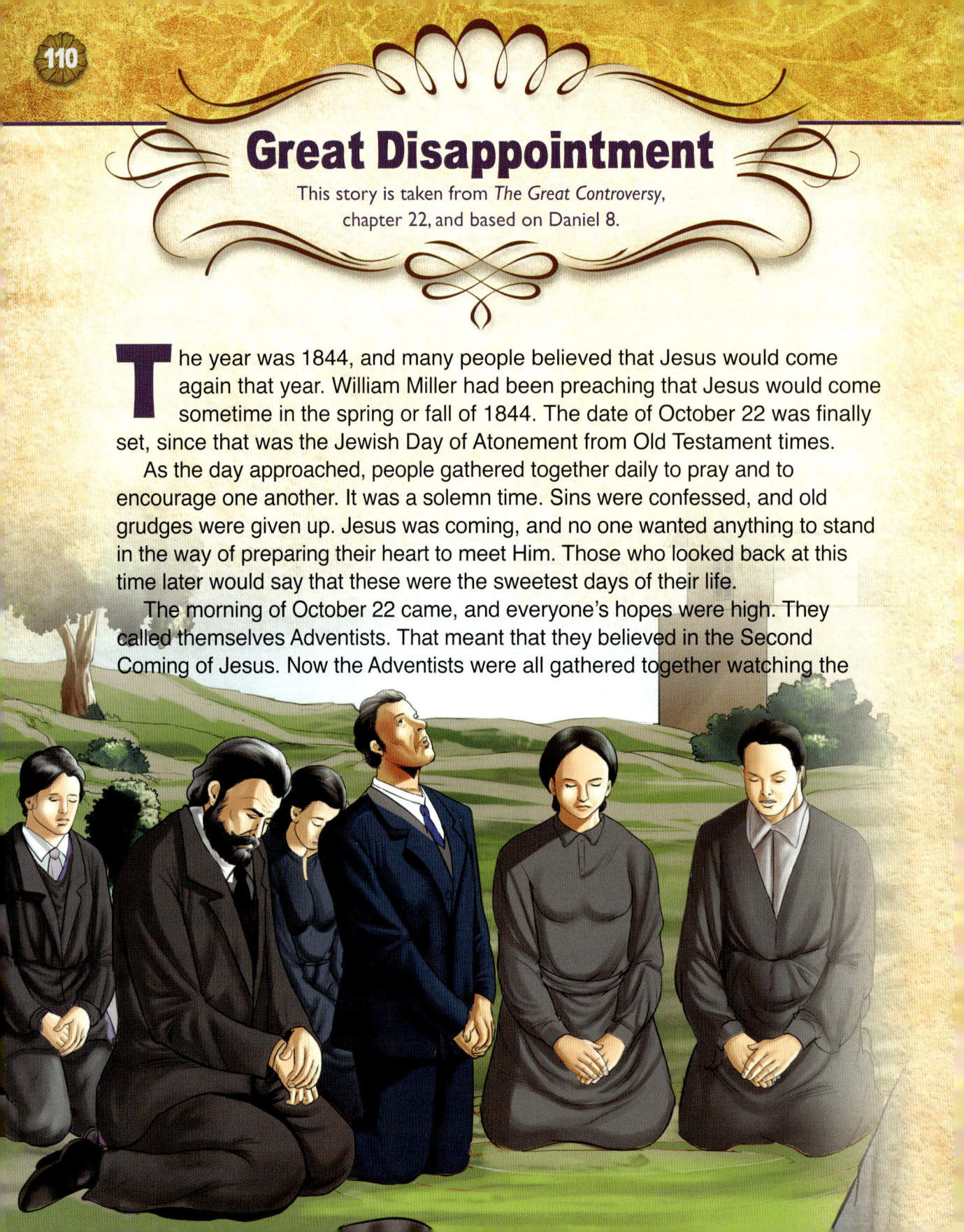

Great Disappointment

This story is taken from *The Great Controversy*, chapter 22, and based on Daniel 8.

The year was 1844, and many people believed that Jesus would come again that year. William Miller had been preaching that Jesus would come sometime in the spring or fall of 1844. The date of October 22 was finally set, since that was the Jewish Day of Atonement from Old Testament times.

As the day approached, people gathered together daily to pray and to encourage one another. It was a solemn time. Sins were confessed, and old grudges were given up. Jesus was coming, and no one wanted anything to stand in the way of preparing their heart to meet Him. Those who looked back at this time later would say that these were the sweetest days of their life.

The morning of October 22 came, and everyone's hopes were high. They called themselves Adventists. That meant that they believed in the Second Coming of Jesus. Now the Adventists were all gathered together watching the eastern sky for the cloud on which Jesus would come. Afternoon came, and then evening, but still Jesus did not come. When midnight passed, there was great weeping among those who had watched and waited all day.

> As the day approached, people gathered together daily to pray and to encourage one another. It was a solemn time.

Dawn broke the next day, and it seemed as if all joy had gone out of their lives. Jesus had not come, and the pain of this experience seemed greater than they could bear.

But the disappointment that they felt was not greater than that which the disciples felt the week of Jesus' crucifixion. They had marched into Jerusalem with Jesus on a donkey. They had waved palm branches and sung, "Blessed is He who comes in the name of the Lord!" They had hoped to see Jesus crowned the Messiah King.

Then just a few days later their hopes were dashed to pieces when Jesus was nailed to the cross. The Son of God had died, and the sorrow that they experienced broke their hearts. That was the worst day of their lives, but better times were coming.

Jesus would arise from the dead three days later, and they would go on to spread the gospel for Him like wildfire!

And that's exactly what happened to the Advent Christians when October 22 had passed. Their faith in God would survive. They would come through stronger in spirit than they had been before they had experienced such great disappointment.

Many who had hoped and waited for Jesus to come now made fun of the Adventists. They said that they had never really believed it would happen. Jesus' failure to come was a relief for them, and His delay now gave them every excuse they needed to let their faith in God die.

However, the faithful few refused to give up, and many questions crowded their minds. Why hadn't Jesus come? Had they made a mistake in their calculations? Was there some Bible verse that could explain the reasons for their disappointment, and should they set yet another date for His appearing?

As the Adventists talked, prayed, and studied, the Holy Spirit helped them to understand that the date was not their error. Then it must be that the event itself was not right. They wondered, "If so, then what was it that had actually happened on October 22, 1844?"

On the morning of October 23, Hiram Edson and several other Advent believers met in his granary to pray. They were so discouraged, and they prayed that God would give them light in their hour of trial. When they finished their prayer meeting, the men went home. As Hiram and a friend were walking through a cornfield, he was impressed with an idea that no one in the group had thought of before.

"The cleansing of the sanctuary" might not be the destruction of this earth by fire, as William Miller had taught. It might be that it had nothing at all to do with the Second Coming of Jesus to earth or the burning of the earth with fire. It might instead mean that Jesus was moving from the Holy Place to the Most Holy Place in the heavenly sanctuary. Edson shared this idea with two friends named Owen Crosier and Dr. Hahn in the nearby town of Canandaigua, New York.

Jesus had not come, and the pain of this experience seemed greater than they could bear.

These men then studied all the Scriptures that they could find about the sanctuary in the Bible and realized it was true. Jesus had become our High Priest in the heavenly sanctuary when He went back to heaven after His resurrection. Then, as Daniel had said, in 1844 Jesus went into the Most Holy Place of the sanctuary to begin what we call the "investigative judgment." It is in the Most Holy Place where Jesus and God are now reviewing the lives of everyone who has chosen to serve God.

God helped His people get through this difficult time. Jesus had not come, but that was all right. God was still with His people, and He would help them spread the good news that Jesus is going to come again soon.

Our Prayer:

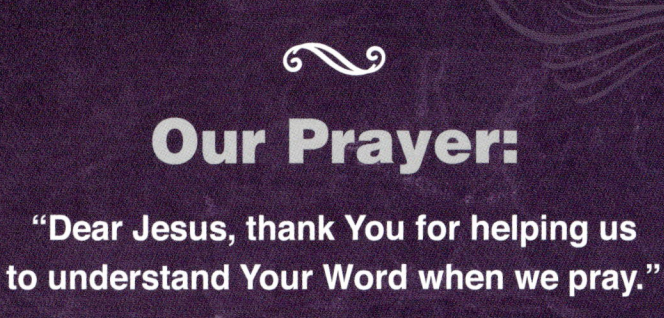

"Dear Jesus, thank You for helping us to understand Your Word when we pray."

Hidden Treasure Questions:

- ✓ Why were the Advent believers so disappointed on October 22, 1844?

- ✓ What did Hiram Edson suggest had actually happened on October 22, 1844?

Listen to this story online!

Scan for bonus content

God Gives a Long Look Into the Future

This story is taken from *The Great Controversy*, chapters 23 and 24, and based on Daniel 8 and 9.

How would you like to know what is coming in the future? "That's not possible," you might say. "No one can know for sure what is coming a year from now, or next week, or even tomorrow." That is true for human beings, and even angels, but there is Someone who can see the future. It is God, and He has given us lots of information in the Bible about the future. We call it prophecy.

Prophecy is one way that God gives information to us, and He usually does it through a prophet. This information can come through the Holy Spirit in a vision or dream. Sometimes an angel of God may deliver the message, and sometimes it is brought to us by God Himself. Daniel received prophetic messages from God in all of these ways.

There are many prophecies found in the Bible. There are hundreds, in fact, and they were all given to tell people what was going to happen in the future.

Some were warnings of bad things to come, such as Noah's prophecy that a flood would destroy the earth. Some were predictions of good things that would happen, such as the birth of the Messiah. Some were very short prophecies, such as the ones that the angels gave to warn the people that Sodom was going to be destroyed. Others were very long, such as the 70-year prophecy that told everyone when the Jews would be coming back to Jerusalem after their captivity in Babylon.

> **There are many prophecies found in the Bible. They were all given to tell people what was going to happen in the future.**

Then there are prophecies that include a timeline. Those prophecies have a timeline because they last so long, and there are many things happening along that time span from start to finish.

The longest timeline prophecy in the Bible is the 2,300-day prophecy. Actually, the 2,300 days stand for 2,300 years, according to biblical interpretation (Ezekiel 4:6). Now, that is a long, long time!

We find this prophecy in the eighth and ninth chapters of Daniel, and it comes in two sections: a smaller time span of 70 weeks (or 490 years) and a second time span of 1,810 years. The first part of the prophecy began when King Artaxerxes gave the "command to restore and build Jerusalem" in 457 B.C. and stretched into the future until the "Messiah the Prince" arrived on the scene (Daniel 9:25). We all know that Jesus was the Messiah, so the 490 years must have ended when Jesus was on earth.

The 490 years take us through A.D. 27, when Jesus was baptized. It continues until A.D. 31, when Jesus died on the cross for you and me. It finally ends in A.D. 34, when Stephen was stoned. That is when God rejected the Jews from being His chosen people and the gospel began to go to the Gentiles (Daniel 9:26, 27). This is really an amazing timeline considering that it was predicted almost 500 years before it was fulfilled.

The second section of this prophecy began in A.D. 34 and ran 1,810 years until 1844.

> **In 1844, Jesus went into the Most Holy Place of the heavenly sanctuary. There He began the last phase of His ministry.**

So what happened in 1844? According to Daniel 8:14, the sanctuary would be cleansed at the end of the 2,300 years. What does that mean?

In 1844, Jesus went into the Most Holy Place of the heavenly sanctuary. There He began the last phase of His ministry as our High Priest before the judgment throne of God. Right now Jesus is in heaven looking at the names of everyone on earth. He is looking to see if you and I have made a choice for Him and want to be saved eternally. He is telling the universe that His blood on Calvary paid for your sins and mine. When He is done doing that, the cleansing of the sanctuary in heaven will be complete, and Jesus will come again!

That is what the 2,300-day prophecy is all about. It is about Jesus coming to die for us according to the timeline. It is about 1844 and Jesus' job as our High Priest in the heavenly sanctuary. It is about the last days of earth's history and Jesus' Second Coming! What an incredible blessing that God would take the time to tell us all about this amazing prophecy in the Bible!

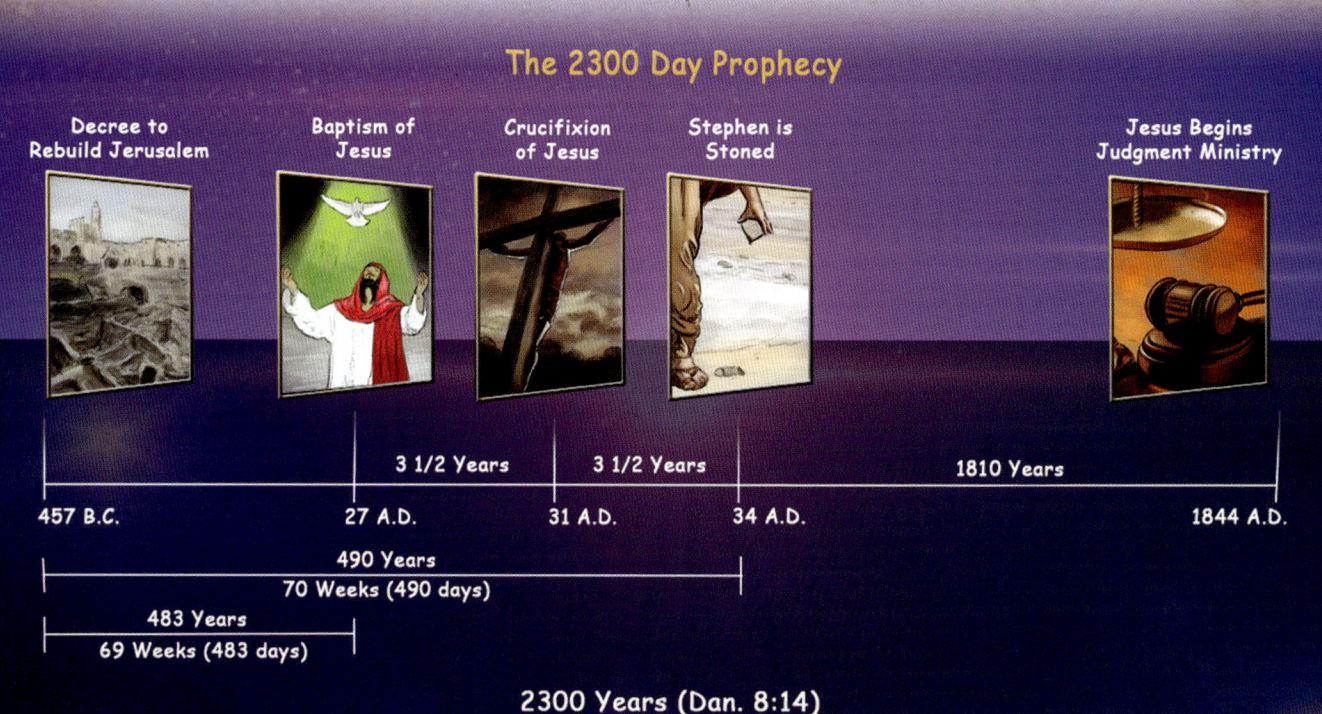

The 2300 Day Prophecy

Decree to Rebuild Jerusalem	Baptism of Jesus	Crucifixion of Jesus	Stephen is Stoned	Jesus Begins Judgment Ministry
457 B.C.	27 A.D.	31 A.D.	34 A.D.	1844 A.D.

- 457 B.C. → 27 A.D.
- 27 A.D. → 31 A.D.: 3 1/2 Years
- 31 A.D. → 34 A.D.: 3 1/2 Years
- 34 A.D. → 1844 A.D.: 1810 Years

490 Years / 70 Weeks (490 days)

483 Years / 69 Weeks (483 days)

2300 Years (Dan. 8:14)

Our Prayer:

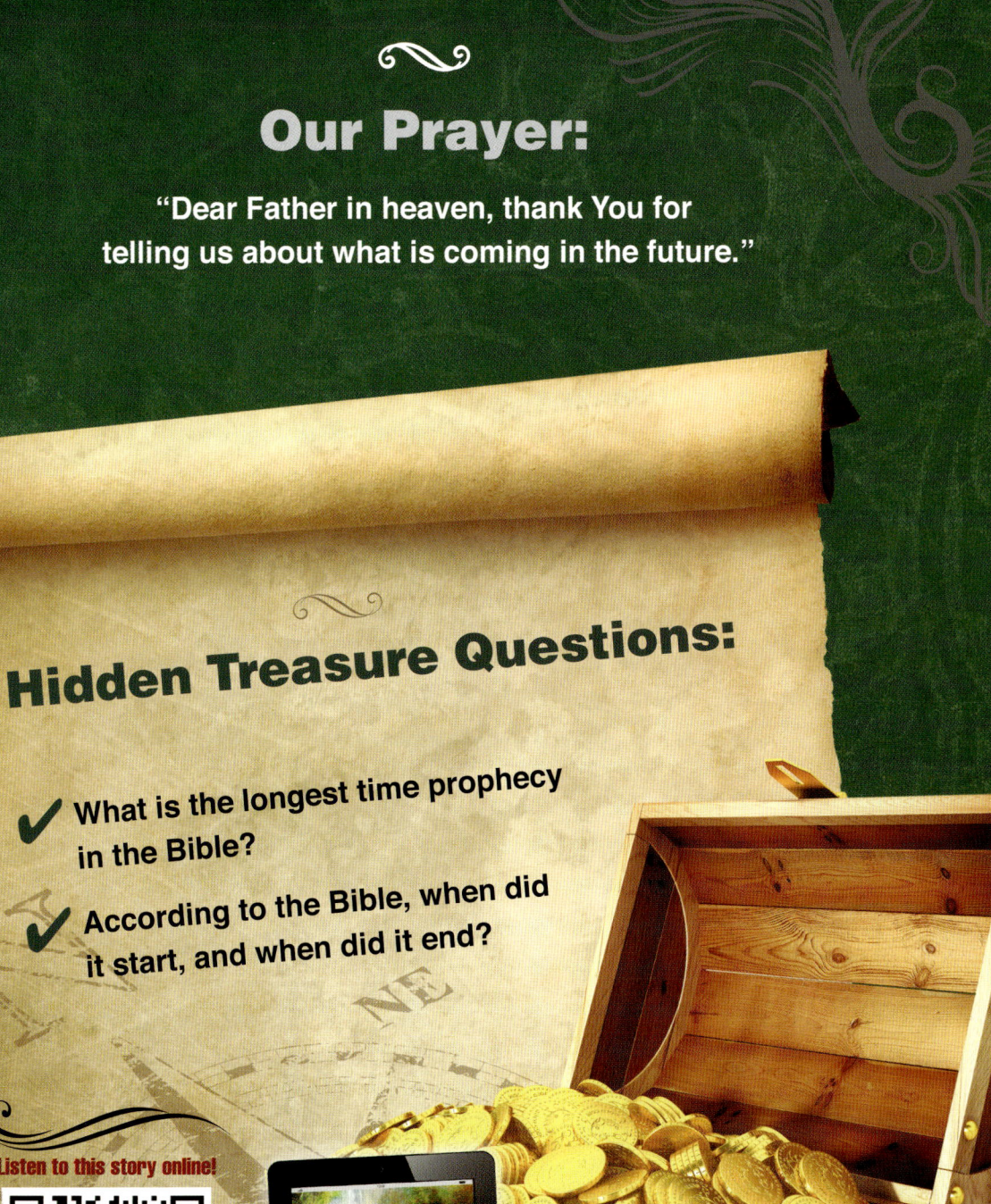

"Dear Father in heaven, thank You for telling us about what is coming in the future."

Hidden Treasure Questions:

✓ What is the longest time prophecy in the Bible?

✓ According to the Bible, when did it start, and when did it end?

Listen to this story online!

Scan for bonus content

God's Special Day

This story is taken from *The Great Controversy*, chapter 26, and based on Genesis 2; Ezekiel 20; and Isaiah 58, 66.

Everyone has a day each year that is special to them. To some, it is Christmas or Thanksgiving or Independence Day. To others, it is an anniversary of some kind, and for many it is their birthday. Birthdays are important, because they are unique and are a celebration of an important time in our lives.

The Sabbath is important to God because it is like a birthday to celebrate the very first week on earth. It was designed to be a day when Adam and Eve and all God's people would remember the wonderful world that God had created for them. The book of Genesis tells us that "God blessed the seventh day and sanctified it, because in it He rested from all His work which God had created and made" (Genesis 2:3).

But there is more. The Sabbath is God's promise or covenant to spend special time with us, if we will spend it with Him. He says, "I also gave them My Sabbaths, to be a sign between them and Me, that they might know that I am the Lord who sanctifies them" (Ezekiel 20:12).

The Sabbath was intended to mean as much to God's people as it did to God. And it seemed to at first. But as more and more people inhabited the earth, all the wonderful things that God did for the people meant less and less to them, including the Sabbath. Soon almost no one was keeping the Sabbath anymore. So God came down to Mt. Sinai and reminded His people: "Remember the Sabbath day, to keep it holy…. the seventh day is the Sabbath of the Lord your God" (Exodus 20:8-10).

Yet God knew that sometimes His people still wouldn't understand just how important the Sabbath was, so He gave them the miracle of the manna. Here's the story.

When the Israelites were wandering in the desert for 40 years, every morning God rained down manna from heaven for them to eat. It was a wonderful blessing, but any manna that was not eaten by the end of each day spoiled. However, on Fridays He gave them twice as much manna so they wouldn't have to gather any on Sabbath. And amazingly, it never spoiled during the Sabbath hours. That's the miracle of the manna, and it showed how special God wanted the Sabbath to be for the Hebrews.

He wants the Sabbath to be special for us, too. He wants us to have a rest day from all the things that wear us out, such as school, chores, and even sports. He wants the Sabbath to be a time when we can bring our families back together to relax with Him.

The Sabbath is a day for singing, praying, and worshipping God in His house.

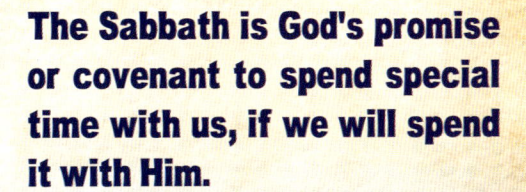

The Sabbath is God's promise or covenant to spend special time with us, if we will spend it with Him.

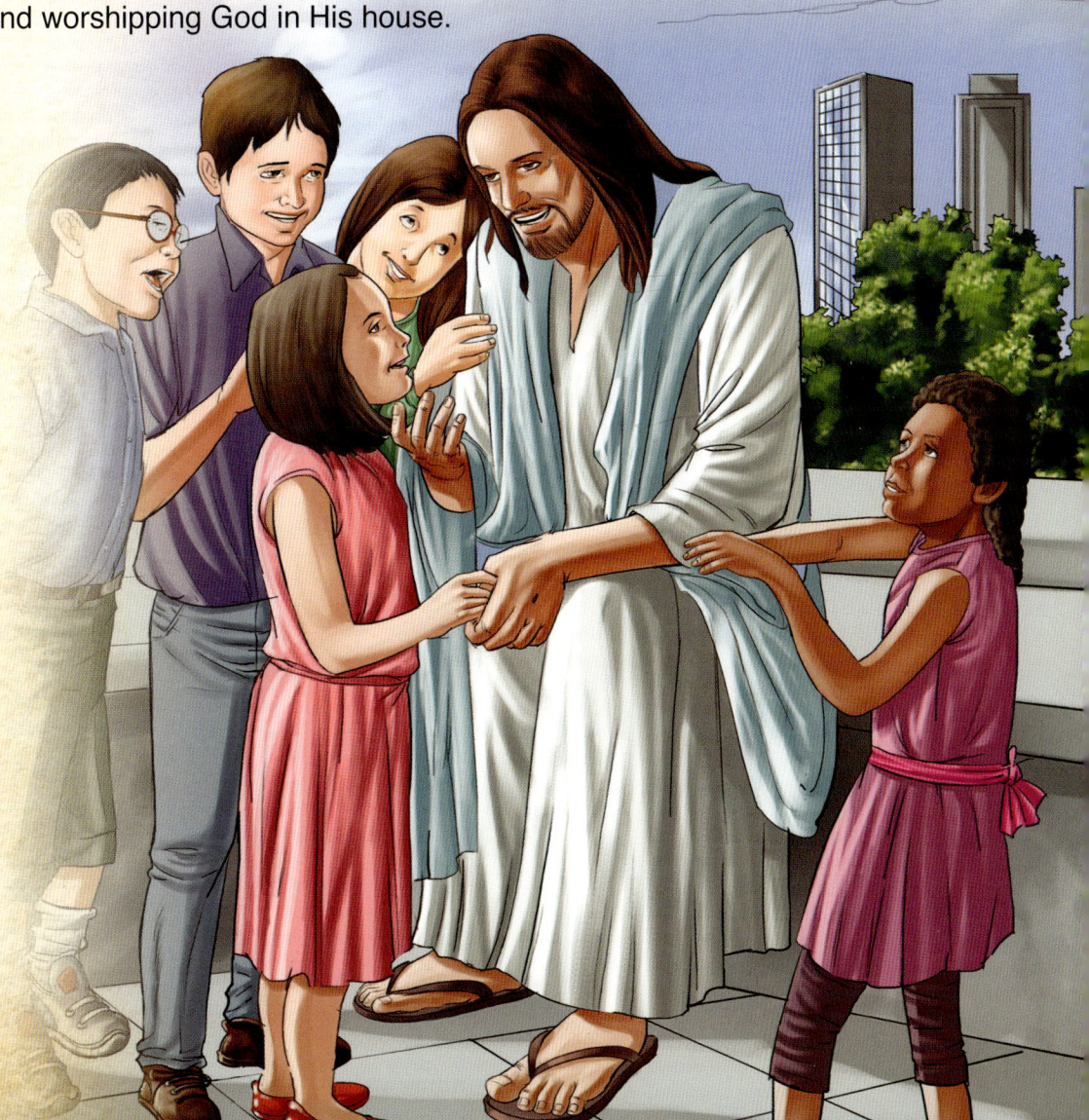

He wants us to use the day to get to know Him better at church, to thank Him for all the blessings He has given us, and to ask His help for the tough times in our life.

Satan tries to get us to forget the Sabbath. He convinces some of us that going to church on the Sabbath day is not important. He fools some people into thinking that the Sabbath is a time for us to do as we please. Others, he persuades to give up the Sabbath completely.

However, if we are God's children and we want Him to be a part of our life, then we need to be in church on the Sabbath. The Bible tells us that is what Jesus did. "As His custom was, He went into the synagogue on the Sabbath day" (Luke 4:16).

If we really love God and want His blessings in our life, we need to respect His Sabbath day and treat it with reverence. "If you turn away your foot from the Sabbath, from doing your pleasure on My holy day, and call the Sabbath a delight, the holy day of the Lord honorable, and shall honor Him, not doing your own ways, nor finding your own pleasure, nor speaking your own words, then you shall delight yourself in the Lord" (Isaiah 58:13, 14).

Most important, if we are planning on living with Jesus someday in our heavenly home, the Sabbath should be the most important day in our lives. "'And it shall come to pass… from one Sabbath to another, all flesh shall come to worship before Me,' says the Lord" (Isaiah 66:23).

That means that when we get to heaven, we will be keeping the Sabbath holy forever. God doesn't want us to wait until then. He wants us to start keeping it right here, right now. Let's start honoring God by spending that special time with Him on His special day.

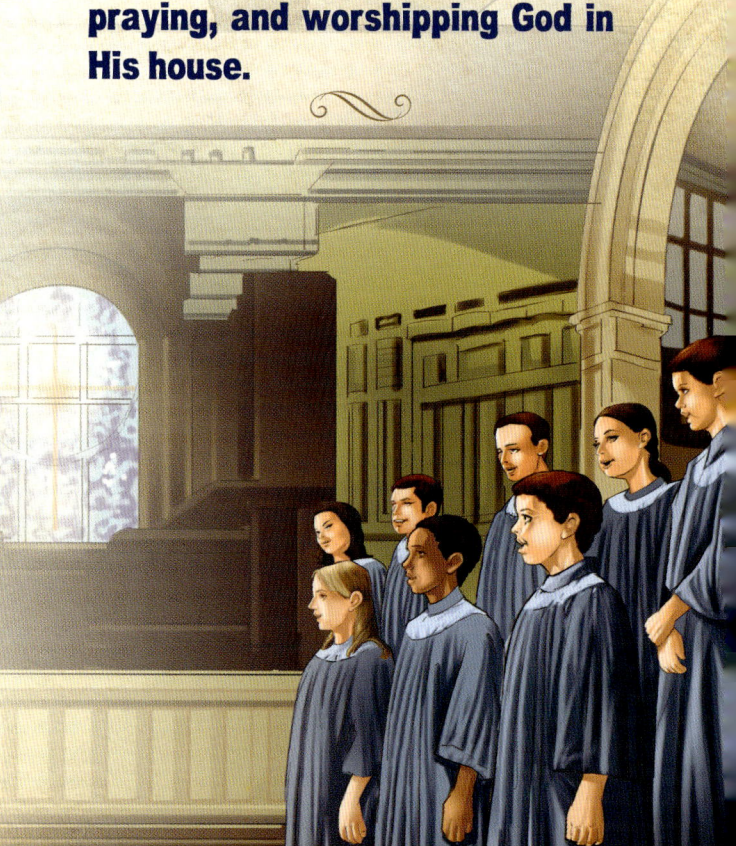

The Sabbath is a day for singing, praying, and worshipping God in His house.

Our Prayer:

"Dear God, thank You so much for the Sabbath. It's the best blessing of all."

Hidden Treasure Questions:

- ✓ On which day of Creation did God make the Sabbath?
- ✓ How did God use manna to show the Israelites how important the Sabbath should be?

Listen to this story online!

Scan for bonus content

What's Going On in the Courts of Heaven?

This story is taken from *The Great Controversy*, chapter 28, and based on Daniel 8.

When someone breaks the law, the police come to the scene of a crime. They question witnesses, take notes and photographs, and see if they can decide what actually happened. Sometimes even a detective shows up to look at all the evidence, and if lawyers get involved, they do an investigation and go to trial.

That is what happened when Lucifer rebelled in heaven. He broke the law of God, but claimed that he wasn't guilty. Then he tricked Adam and Eve by lying to them about God, and dragged the entire human race into the crimes that he was committing. Before long most people in this world were thinking that Satan was right and God was wrong.

God tried many ways to show people that He is fair, loving, and good. One way He did this was to set up a sanctuary where people could come to worship and see exactly what He was doing to save the world. The sanctuary on earth was a copy of the one in heaven, and everything in the sanctuary had a purpose. The furniture, the Holy Place, the Most Holy Place, and even the clothes for the priests were all designed to show how God's plan of salvation works to save us from sin.

Every day the priests offered incense in the Holy Place and filled the seven-branched candlestick with oil. Weekly they brought into this room 12 new loaves of flatbread for the priests. They also sprinkled the blood there when an animal was sacrificed for the whole nation.

These ceremonies pointed to all the important parts of salvation for the human race. The incense represented the prayers of God's people, and the light from the candlestick represented His light to all the world. The bread represented Jesus, who is our spiritual food, and the animal sacrifices represented the death of Jesus on the cross.

Once a year, on the Day of Atonement, the high priest brought the blood from a special goat into the Most Holy Place and sprinkled it in front of God's ark. This showed that God's people and the sanctuary were being cleansed from sin.

Years later when Jesus died on the cross, He fulfilled the prophecies that pointed to Him as the Lamb that takes away the sins of the world. Then when He ascended to heaven in A.D. 31, He went into the Holy Place of the heavenly sanctuary to serve as High Priest for the human race and to answer the prayers of His people. During this time Satan has been condemning God's people, saying that they are not worthy of His love and forgiveness. However, Jesus' death on the cross paid for their sins, and He has been reminding Satan that the blood of His righteousness makes them as white as snow.

Then in 1844, Jesus' job in the heavenly sanctuary changed. That year was the end of the 2,300-day prophecy in Daniel 8, when Jesus started the last part of His ministry as our Savior. We sometimes call this period of time the investigative judgment. It means that Jesus is reviewing the lives of everyone who has ever lived on this earth, those who

God tried many ways to show people that He is fair, loving, and good. One way He did this was to set up a sanctuary.

served God and those who persecuted His people. Those who were not enemies of God have been marked by the angels to be raised on the resurrection morning.

Those of us who are living are also being examined by God to see if we have accepted Jesus as our Savior and been forgiven of our sins. If we have, then our record is clean, and we are sealed for a place in heaven. This seal is God's stamp of approval and means that He can trust us to go to heaven and not cause trouble, as Lucifer did.

If we have accepted Jesus as our Savior, then our record is clean.

If we are not given a clean record, it means that we have not been covered by Jesus' blood because we have not asked Him to cleanse us of every sin. It means that we like the things of this world more than we want to be with Jesus in heaven. That means we will not get to live with Him forever, but must die when He comes again because "the wages of sin is death" (Romans 6:23).

What a shame that would be. We know that Jesus loved us so much that He died to save us from our sins. We know that He is in the heavenly sanctuary as our High Priest helping us to fight against Satan's temptations. We know that He wants to make us as white as snow, if we will just surrender our lives to Him.

"The gift of God is eternal life," and Jesus wants to give it to us. Why not accept that gift today?

Our Prayer:

"Dear Jesus, thank You for being my High Priest in heaven to cover all my sins with Your blood."

Hidden Treasure Questions:

✓ What year did Jesus enter the Most Holy Place in the heavenly sanctuary?

✓ What do we call the part of Jesus' ministry in heaven when He is checking on you and me?

Listen to this story online!

Scan for bonus content

The Greatest Battle

This story is taken from *The Great Controversy*, chapter 29-32, and based on Revelation 12, 20; Ezekiel 28; Genesis 3; and Acts 2.

There is a great battle going on between good and evil. Every human being is a part of it, whether we want to be or not. Those who are good want to obey God, and those who do evil follow Satan.

But it wasn't always that way. Long ago in heaven there was only happiness and harmony. Every creature throughout the entire universe adored God and worshipped Him as the Creator. No one imagined that evil could find a home in God's universe, because everything was perfect and filled with peace and love.

Then one day Lucifer upset the joy of heaven by questioning God's goodness. He wanted to prove that God's laws were unfair and that no one could keep the rules of heaven. He even challenged Jesus for His throne beside the Father. Many angels took Lucifer's side, although the majority did not.

Finally, a war broke out in heaven. Michael and His angels fought with Satan, and Satan was thrown out of heaven. He went to the created beings of other worlds and tried to convince them that God was mean and unfair. But no one would listen to him. Finally, he came to earth, a new world that God had just created, and here he found a home.

Adam and Eve were his next victims. With evil skill, Satan tempted them to believe his lies about God, and they ate the forbidden fruit. They made a bad decision and believed Satan's lies. Because of this, the young couple were sent away from the garden and the tree of life. Without the fruit from the tree of life, Adam and Eve would eventually die.

Satan was delighted that he had convinced Adam and Eve to sin. He rejoiced that he had caused such great sadness in heaven over the loss of God's children.

Our first parents were very sorry for doubting God and begged Him to let them

> **Finally, a war broke out in heaven. Michael and His angels fought with Satan, and he was thrown out of heaven.**

go back to their garden home. But God said that it was impossible. They were sinners, and their sin had brought heartache and misery into the world. If they were allowed to eat the fruit from the tree of life, sin with all its pain would never end.

However, God never stopped loving Adam and Eve, and He wanted them to know that. So God the Father promised them that Jesus would one day come to live in this world and die for the human race. Jesus' sacrifice would pay for the sins of God's children, and they would one day have their garden home back.

Our first parents were very sorry for doubting God and begged Him to let them go back to their garden home. But God said that it was impossible.

To remind our first parents about the price this would cost, God asked them to sacrifice a little lamb on an altar. This lamb represented Jesus, the Lamb of God, who would redeem them from sin.

But for now Adam and Eve, through the power of Jesus, would have to work hard and fight against the temptations of the evil one. They would suffer pain and sadness and one day would die and be buried in a grave.

Years passed, and the earth became wicked. People grew violent, and their thoughts were only evil continually. It seemed as if Satan had triumphed over God. He had turned God's earth into a battleground between good and evil, and evil was winning.

God decided that He would have to destroy the earth with water, or His plan of salvation would never come to pass. Noah built an ark to save those who would choose to escape the coming flood, but only eight people got aboard. When the flood came, every trace of Satan's wicked civilization disappeared.

The human race had to start all over again in a new world. Times were hard, but God had promised that He would be with them. Unfortunately, once again Satan turned the hearts of men and women against God. By the time Abraham was born, almost no one worshipped God. But God chose this man to be the father of a chosen nation.

Israel was given the task of showing the world what God can do for a nation when they serve Him faithfully. He gave the Israelites His Ten Commandments to share with the whole world, but they failed Him miserably. Again and again, they fell away from His plan for them. They worshipped idols, ignored the holy Sabbath, and killed God's prophets who were sent with messages of warning. Once again, it seemed as if Satan was winning the war between good and evil.

By the time Jesus came to earth, Israel no longer understood what God had called them to do. They were supposed to be letting their light shine so that they could win people for the kingdom of God. Instead, they made the commandments of God a burden to bear.

Jesus tried to show them the love of the Father by doing many wonderful miracles, but they refused to believe that He was the Son of God. They ignored the signs from heaven and killed the spotless Lamb of God.

For the universe looking on, it seemed as if Satan had finally won. He had crucified the Creator of heaven and earth. Now if he could keep Jesus in the grave, he felt sure that his plan to overthrow the world would be complete.

But, of course, that was impossible. Jesus was God, and God cannot lose the war between good and evil. Jesus arose from the tomb to conquer death and the grave. A few days later, He went to heaven to be our great High Priest in the heavenly sanctuary.

Back in Jerusalem, the Holy Spirit was giving the disciples power to take the gospel to the world, and they did just that. The followers of Jesus went to the four corners of the earth spreading the story of salvation.

Satan was furious! He had hoped to kill Jesus, but now the disciples were doing even more amazing things to show the world that God is love.

Down through the ages, Satan has tried desperately to destroy the church. Sometimes he has used fierce persecution from outside the church, even torturing and killing Christians to get them to give up their faith in Jesus. Other times, he has used false teachings and corruption within the church. His goal is always the same. It is to convince people to turn away from Jesus and follow him.

One day soon this terrible war between good and evil will be over. Satan may seem to win a battle from time to time, but God has already won the war. When Jesus died on the cross, this spelled the end of Satan and his evil kingdom.

God has already won the war. When Jesus died on the cross, this spelled the end of Satan.

When Jesus comes again, God's children will be taken to heaven. We will be free from Satan and will never have to listen to his lies and temptations again. And when the judgment day is over, Satan and his demons will be destroyed in the lake of fire. Sin and sinners will be no more. Adam and Eve will be given back their garden home, and the great controversy between good and evil will be over.

Our Prayer:

"Dear Father, help us to be faithful to You in the war between good and evil."

Hidden Treasure Questions:

✓ Who started the battle between good and evil in heaven?

✓ What are two different ways that Satan has tried to destroy God's church?

Listen to this story online!

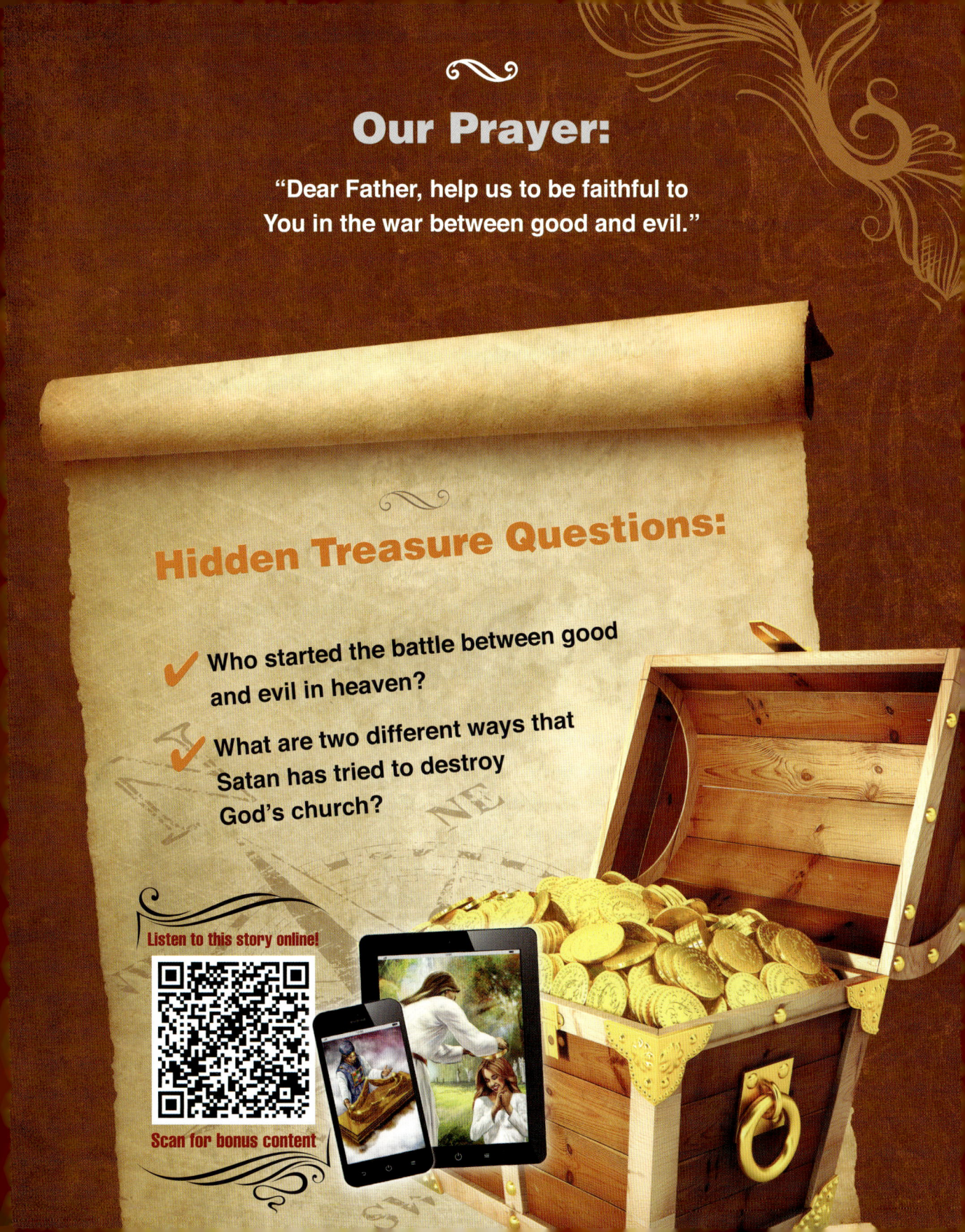

Scan for bonus content

Satan's Deadly Tricks

This story is taken from
The Great Controversy, chapter 32.

The time is drawing near for Jesus to come, and Satan knows it. He knows that his chances to deceive the world will soon be gone.

He doesn't want us to be saved and taken to heaven where he once lived, so he tries to deceive us and trick us into believing his lies.

More than anything, he wants to discourage us and make us feel sad when everything is going wrong. That is exactly the time when we should pray. Satan knows that through prayer we get our help from God. He knows that if we pray, asking God to direct our lives, we will win all our battles against him. So he tries to keep us from going to our knees and praying. Satan knows that some of us will pray no matter what he does, so he often tries to falsely use prayer as a weapon against us. When we pray for help from God, Satan sends us troubles so that we will be tempted to think that prayer doesn't help. Then he tries to get us to give up our faith in God.

There are other ways that Satan tries to deceive people too. He wants people to think that smart people in this world sometimes know more than the Bible does. Without God's Spirit to help them understand what they are reading in the Bible, some people become critics of it. But since God created science, He has the real answers, and He will show us the right ones if we are patient.

Satan will try to do everything he can to get you to doubt God's Word, the Bible. Sometimes there may be things that you do not understand, and he will try to make you wonder if God's Word is true. But God's Word is always true, no matter what any person may say. He has given us many truths in the Bible that are not hard to understand, and they will always stay the same. We need to be faithful in studying and doing the things we can understand, and then God will help us to understand even more things.

Sometimes we read things in the Bible that we don't want to hear. Instead of humbly obeying God's Word, we try to think of reasons that we should not have to do as God asks. This is one of Satan's biggest temptations. Satan knows that he can probably never get us to ignore the really big things in the Bible, so he gets us to look at the little things. Satan uses all of these things to distract us, trick us, and get us to disobey God. We need to remember that if God says we should or should not do something, we need to obey Him. We owe Him that much. After all, He is our Creator.

Today, more than ever before, people don't believe that Satan exists. They think that he is make-believe, and they create pictures of him to let people think that he is a fairy tale. But, of course, this is just another big lie that Satan uses to deceive us.

Many kinds of meditation do not encourage people to use the Bible, and that can be very dangerous.

In almost the opposite way, Satan tries to communicate with people who think he does exist and who believe in him in the wrong way. He does this through many things that use evil power from the supernatural world. It might be a séance, where people think that they can talk to the dead, or possibly in books, movies, or games through which demons from the spirit world can deceive us.

Satan tries to deceive us through books, movies, or games through which demons from the spirit world can communicate.

Finally, Satan tries to deceive us by destroying our confidence in the Bible. He does this by getting people to find fault with the Bible. For example, he gets people to say that the Bible is not consistent. He says that the Bible tells us one thing in one part and then says the opposite in another. This is just another lie that Satan uses so that we will not trust the Bible. Then people use this to discourage others and excuse themselves from understanding the Bible, or maybe studying it at all.

Satan uses all of these things to deceive us and to get us to give up our faith in God. However, Jesus died so that we might overcome Satan, as He did when He was here on earth. We can thank God for that.

Our Prayer:

"Dear Jesus, help me to listen to Your voice so that I can avoid Satan's temptations."

Hidden Treasure Questions:

- ✓ What are some ways that Satan tries to deceive Christians today?
- ✓ When we pray for help from God, what does Satan do?

Listen to this story online!

Scan for bonus content

What Happens When We Die?

This story is taken from *The Great Controversy*, chapter 33, 34, and based on Genesis 3; Ecclesiates. 9; Romans 6; John 11; I Corinthians 15; and I Thessalonians 4.

Many people ask, "What happens when we die? Where do we go, and what do we do when we get there? Is heaven a real place, and have those who died gone there before us? If they were not such a good person, what happens to them? Will they end up somewhere else such as hell?"

We know of only a few people in history who have come back from the dead, and they were raised to life by the power of God. Some, such as Moses and the ones who rose up with Jesus on His resurrection day, went to heaven a short time later. We have no record of any conversations that they had while in heaven with people back on earth.

The stories in the Old Testament about the two little boys raised by Elijah and Elisha tell us nothing about what these boys saw or felt after they died. The widow's son in Nain, Jairus' daughter, and Lazarus didn't say a thing about life after death either, and Jesus Himself raised them to life. If there had been something to say about it, surely they would have told us! Such fantastic stories would be headlines for sure in today's newspapers and Internet news sites.

But these people didn't tell us anything, which leads us to only one conclusion. There was nothing to tell. They did not see, hear, or feel anything, because death is a quiet sleep for those who have stopped living here on earth (John 11:11-14).

For centuries, Satan has been spreading the lie that when we die, we actually go on living. "You will not surely die," he said to Eve in the Garden of Eden (Genesis 3:4).

Satan wants us to believe that the dead go on living, and that we can talk to them.

Why would Satan start such a story? Why would he spread such a lie? Well, for one thing, he wants us to believe that we can go on living, no matter what we do in this life, even if it is bad. He wants us to believe that there will be no price to pay for living a sinful life. However, God has told us, "The wages of sin is death" (Romans 6:23).

The Bible says that the dead know nothing. However, Satan would like us to believe that dead people continue to live in heaven or hell, or places such as limbo or purgatory. The Church of Rome taught that limbo was a place where the spirits of dead people floated around waiting for a body to live in. They said that if bad people want to be in heaven, they must pay for all their sins, so they must first go to purgatory when they die.

The Bible is very clear about what happens to people when they die. "For the living know that they will die; but the dead know nothing, and they have no more reward, for the memory of them is forgotten. Also their love, their hatred, and their envy have now perished; nevermore will they have a share in anything done under the sun" (Ecclesiastes 9:5, 6).

Apart from God we cannot exist, because we are sinful creatures. Even the holy angels of heaven cannot live without God. He is their Creator and Sustainer. Only God lives eternally, because He is the source of all life. He is the Master Designer of all things and the One who holds the universe in His hands (1 Timothy 6:15, 16).

When Jesus raises all God's people to life, everyone will come out of their graves. The good giants who lived before Noah's flood will be resurrected. The good people who lived for God will wake up, and so will those who have been executed down through the centuries, because they chose to be true to God. And, of course, all the people whom you and I know loved Jesus will wake up to see Him coming again.

Those of us who are still alive will see the angels welcome everyone from their graves. Then we will be changed in an instant, quicker than you can snap your fingers. Soon Jesus will give us robes of light that shine brighter than the noonday sun. We will all look young again, even the old grandmas and grandpas. People who were blind, or in a wheelchair, or had cancer will no longer have these disorders (1 Corinthians 15:51-54).

"Then we who are alive and remain shall be caught up together with them in the clouds to meet the Lord in the air. And thus we shall always be with the Lord" (1 Thessalonians 4:17).

That is a very exciting thing to think about. When that day comes, we will all be very happy, because Jesus will give us a crown of life, and we will live with Him forever and ever.

> **When Jesus raises all God's people to life, everyone will come out of their graves.**

Our Prayer:

"Dear God, I am so glad that You have the power over death and the grave."

Hidden Treasure Questions:

- ✓ What was the very first lie that Satan told Eve?

- ✓ When people go to séances and think that they are talking with the dead, to whom are they really talking?

Listen to this story online!

Scan for bonus content

A Storm Is Coming

This story is taken from *The Great Controversy*, chapter 36, and based on Matthew 24:37; and Luke 21.

Ever since the very beginning of this world, it has been Satan's goal to defeat God in the war between good and evil. From the fall of Adam and Eve in Eden, to the crucifixion of Jesus, to the last days of this world's history, Satan has been at work trying to get you and me to doubt that God loves us.

Every day Satan stalks us "like a roaring lion, seeking whom he may devour" (1 Peter 5:8). As the time draws near for Jesus to come again, we can be sure that he will increase those attacks.

People today want to think that we are smarter than people were in the ancient times of Israel. Satan wants us to believe that we are more civilized and would never worship gods such as Baal or Ashtoreth. He wants us to think that we would never do some of the barbaric things that people did in the days of Elijah.

However, nothing could be further from the truth! We have only exchanged the pagan gods of wood and stone for fashionable things in this world such as cars, homes, jewelry, and bank accounts. What will we sacrifice to get these things? Will we cheat on a test to get a better grade? If someone gives us too much change at the grocery store, will we give it back? It is the little decisions that we make that show the direction we will go when we have to make big decisions.

This world is getting more unsafe to live in every day, and yet many people don't want to be bothered with religious things anymore. They don't want to hear about Jesus in our schools. They don't want to see the Ten Commandments in our courthouses, and they would rather not see the words "In God We Trust" on our money.

> They don't want to hear about Jesus in our schools. They don't want to see the Ten Commandments in our courthouses.

What they don't understand is that without God's laws in our country, this nation would not be a safe place in which to live. We wouldn't want the police to go away, or the judges to let all of the criminals go free, but that is what many people expect God to do. They don't want Him to tell them what to do, and they don't want Him to punish them for all the bad things that they are doing.

So, little by little, people get to the place where they think that they should be able to do whatever they want, whenever they want, and with whomever they want. But we have plenty of examples from history of people who tried that, and the results were disastrous!

The days of Noah were a perfect example, and so were the cities of Sodom and Gomorrah. The people during those times had plenty of money and time to do whatever they wanted, and yet they only became more evil because of it. They did not have God in their lives, and in the end, they were destroyed because their hearts were only evil continually.

A more recent example was the country of France during the French Revolution in the 1790s. The people during those times decided that they didn't want religion or God in their country. So they all became atheists and killed everyone who was a Christian. Because the people had turned their backs on God, Satan could do whatever he wanted with them. Within just a few short years, there were hardly any Christians left in the country. No one trusted anyone, and thousands died by execution under the guillotine. This is what happens when God's Ten Commandments are no longer welcome.

Many people in countries around the world are doing exactly what the people of Sodom and Gomorrah did. They spend money as if there is no tomorrow, and they spend their time doing things that have no eternal value.

> **Natural disasters will become more frequent. Earthquakes will increase, and so will storms, floods, and tidal waves.**

They feel that they should be able to do anything they want and do not want anyone to tell them what is right or wrong. If you do away with the good laws, then anything can happen. Someday people will be treated wrongly because they are trying to do what is right.

But the most shocking thing is that we are just like the people in the days of Noah. Few people in the world today can see the times of trouble that are soon to come upon the world. They do not understand that as evil increases everywhere, God's Spirit will slowly be withdrawn from the world.

Natural disasters will become more frequent. Earthquakes will increase, and so will storms, floods, and tidal waves. In many places, God's people will be blamed for these catastrophes, just as Elijah was blamed for the three years of no rain in Israel. Persecutions will increase for God's people, as they did for the schools of the prophets during the days of Jezebel.

This will be a time when people will worry a lot. People's hearts will fail them for fear of what is coming on the world (Luke 21:26). Just like King Saul in the Old Testament, people will want to know what is coming next and will try to speak with the dead through mediums so that they can find out. They will believe that God's commandments are no longer important.

The deceptions have already begun in preparation for what is coming. The

Bible is being preached less and less, even in churches. Satan is mixing false ideas with Bible truth so that he can trick people into believing his lies. Just like a little poison in food, his deceptions are not noticed at first. That makes them all the more dangerous because people wouldn't eat such spiritual food if they knew that Satan's poison would cost them their eternal life.

It is all very sad. If people would just read their Bibles, they would see the danger that they are in.

Now we must ask ourselves some very important questions. When times get difficult, will we be faithful to the truths found in the Bible? Will we be true to Jesus and obey His commandments? The times that we have been warned about in the Bible are coming very soon. Will we be ready?

The deceptions have already begun in preparation for what is coming. The Bible is being preached less and less, even in churches.

Our Prayer:

"Dear Jesus, help me not to forget how much I need prayer and the Bible every day."

Hidden Treasure Questions:

✓ To what kind of animal does Peter compare Satan?

✓ What are the two big lies that Satan will use to deceive the world before Jesus comes again?

Listen to this story online!

Scan for bonus content

The Amazing Word of God

This story is taken from
The Great Controversy, chapter 37.

The Bible is the oldest book in the world, written by many different kinds of people over a span of 1,500 years. Farmers, fishermen, shepherds, prophets, scholars, tax collectors, generals, preachers, and kings have contributed to this project inspired by the Holy Spirit, and what a road it has traveled! It has weathered the storms of time and been hunted down by kings and emperors. Fire, persecution, and the sword have destroyed it. Today science is trying to do away with the Bible completely as the Word of God.

We should not be surprised that Satan has done everything in his power to destroy the Bible. During the Dark Ages, most people in Europe couldn't read or write, so knowledge of the Bible was scarce. It was a time of castles, moats, and Knights of the Round Table. It was also a time of poverty and disease, when people were so poor that they were bought and sold along with the land they farmed. It was a time of great ignorance and superstition, and it seemed as if the whole world had fallen asleep spiritually. However,

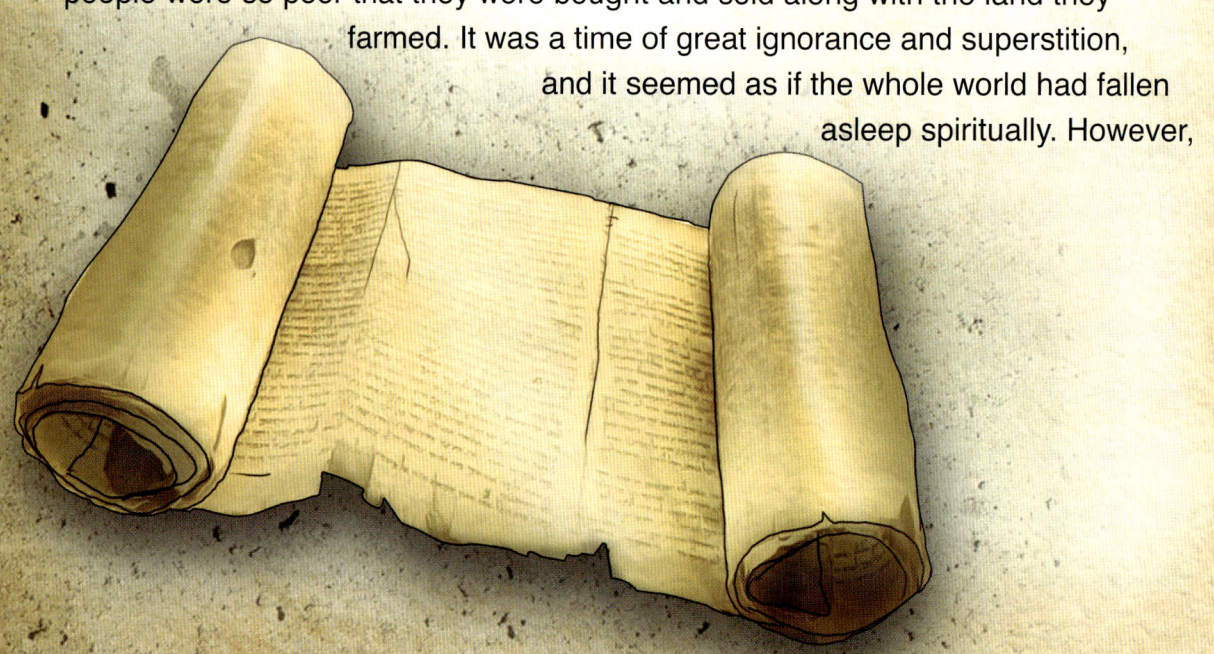

God was not asleep. He has always had a plan by which He could preserve His Scriptures, and has kept a close watch over the copies of His sacred writings. In every age, He has had His champions to keep His Word safe and to make it available to the world. Reformers such as John Wycliffe, Martin Luther, and William Tyndale pioneered the way in bringing the Bible to the world. Standing against the waves of persecution by the state churches, they worked to translate the Scriptures and get them into the hands of the common people. Little by little, the sacrifices of these brave men helped release the chains of spiritual darkness that had held the world in their grasp for so many centuries.

During the years of the Protestant Reformation, the Bible was translated into many languages, and it became available as never before. Things had changed little in the way that Bibles were copied down through the centuries of time, but Johann Gutenberg's invention of block printing changed all of that. Copies of the Bible could now be made much more quickly, helping spread the Word of God, so that people everywhere could have their own Bible.

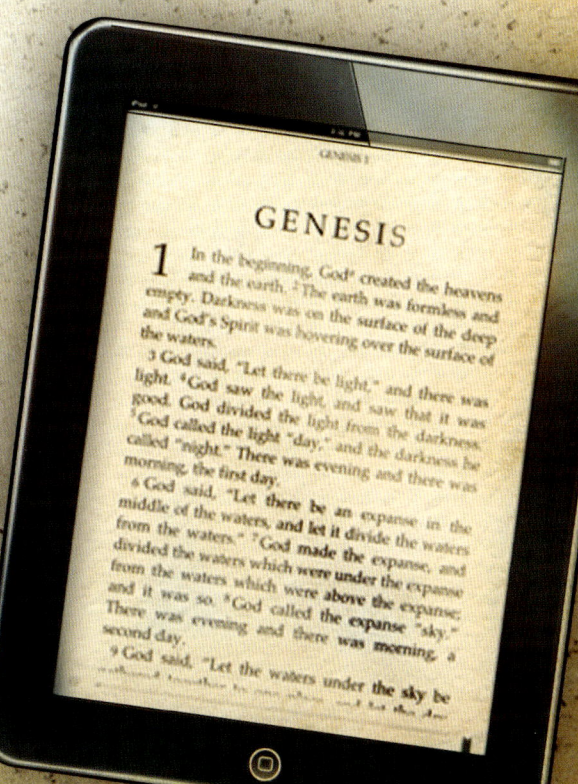

> **God has always had a plan by which He could preserve His Scriptures, and has kept a close watch over the copies of His sacred writings.**

Then a new age of science and scientific discovery dawned. The Industrial Revolution brought sweeping changes in how people lived, worked, and were educated. Inventions began sprouting up everywhere that allowed people to get more done in less time. It was a time of great human accomplishments, and everywhere nations were celebrating amazing progress.

Many began to wonder, Do I need God or the Bible anymore? Are the Scriptures still accurate? Is the Bible even the same book that it was in the days of the early Christian church? How can it possibly be free from mistakes after centuries of translation and change?

However, God is eternal and all-knowing, and His preservation of the Scriptures would continue no matter the obstacles. Startling new discoveries in archaeology helped prove that the Bible is genuine. In 1859, Constantin von Tischendorf, a noted German scholar, discovered a lost copy of an ancient Bible manuscript called the Sinaiticus. The manuscript had been written in the fourth century and is now considered one of the most valuable Bible

In 1948, a collection of ancient manuscripts called the Dead Sea Scrolls was discovered.

manuscripts anywhere in the world. Why? Because it is a complete copy of the New Testament and shows that very little change has taken place in Bible translations down through the years of time.

Then in 1948, a collection of ancient manuscripts called the Dead Sea Scrolls was discovered in several caves in Israel. The scrolls were about 2,000 years old, and in spite of all those years in hiding, they were actually in relatively good shape. The book of Daniel, one of the most disputed books in the Old Testament, was among the scrolls. It was written in Hebrew, with parts of it in Aramaic.

Most important, when the experts translated the Daniel scroll, they found it to be the same as versions of Daniel now used in modern Bibles. Amazing! Here was proof that God's Word is accurate and can be counted on, as Christians have been claiming for centuries. It is comforting to know that the Word of God is just as reliable today as it has always been.

However, with the increase in the world population during the past 200 years, the need to take the gospel to every nation, kindred, tongue, and people has now become more urgent than ever. Of course, God knew that the ways in which the Bible is produced would have to speed up, and He had a plan for that, too. The explosion in knowledge and technology has now put us light-years ahead of handwritten manuscripts and Gutenberg's block printing. High-speed presses churn out Bibles at a speed never before seen in history. Electronic capabilities of laptops, iPads, and satellite phones can access the Word of God in dozens of ways. Today's Internet technology makes information available in ways not thought possible just a generation ago.

Truly, knowledge has increased, and just in time to help take the gospel to all the world for these end times. Bible societies everywhere are working on translations of the Bible so that people in every language on earth can have a copy of the Scriptures to read. Billions of copies of God's Word have now been printed in hundreds of languages, and editions are being taken to every corner of the globe.

Thank God for His precious Word! Today, we can choose to read just about any kind of Bible that we want, with dozens of translations available. We have copies of the Bible in book form, on our phones, and online. But the greatest blessing of the Bible is how the Holy Spirit speaks through it to give us exactly what we need, when we need it.

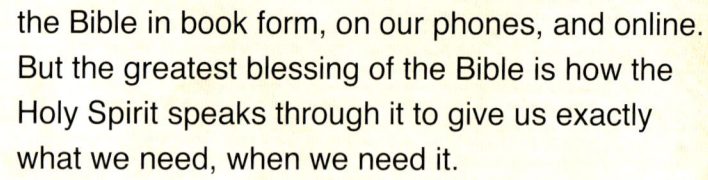

If we treasure the Bible more than fine gold and jewels, we will give it first place among our most valued earthly possessions. Thousands have done just that down through the ages, guarding it at great cost, even giving their lives for it. What a sacrifice they have made for God and His Word! What a gift they have given you and me! We will never know just how blessed we are until we reach heaven! Surely, we must value it above all else in this life as we wait for Jesus to come again.

> **Today, we can choose to read just about any kind of Bible that we want, with dozens of translations available.**

Our Prayer:

"Dear God in heaven, thank You so much for the Bible. You have protected it for so long, and I want to cherish it as the most valuable of all my possessions."

Hidden Treasure Questions:

✓ How many years did it take to write all the books of the Bible?

✓ Who discovered an ancient Bible manuscript from the fourth century?

Listen to this story online!

Scan for bonus content

The Final Warning

This story is taken from *The Great Controversy*, chapter 38, and based on Rev. 14; 12:12; and Matthew 24:42.

Just before Jesus comes again the message of salvation must go everywhere. Jesus said, "This gospel of the kingdom will be preached in all the world as a witness to all the nations, and then the end will come" (Matthew 24:14).

That is what is happening today. The truth is flying like wildfire to every nation, tribe, tongue, and people with the use of Bibles, books, radio, television, and the Internet. The Bible is being printed in the local languages of the mountain tribes in what used to be the cannibal country of Papua New Guinea. Windup radios are being used in the jungles of Brazil. Satellite television is being watched in the cities of India. And the story of salvation can be told on the Internet nearly anywhere in the world.

Soon the Holy Spirit will be fully poured out on God's people, and amazing things will be done to bring the world's attention to the gospel. Demons will be cast out, and people will suddenly speak miraculously in languages that they could never speak before. God's people will perform great miracles, healing the sick, and even raising the dead (Mark 16:17, 18). Some of these things are already happening, but just before Jesus comes, we will see them done in greater numbers by more of God's people in more countries. This will be a sure sign of the times in which we are living. With God's power attending His people, the final warning of the gospel will go to every corner of the world.

The truth is flying like wildfire to every nation, tribe, tongue, and people with the use of Bibles, radio, television, and the Internet.

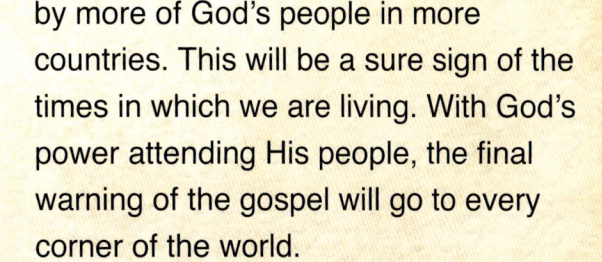

Because Satan knows that his time is short, he will do everything that he can to get Christians to listen to him. If he can, he will cause them to leave God's true churches everywhere. Through his worldly ministers, he is teaching that the Ten Commandments are no longer important. Using television, movies, and books, he is teaching the world that the dead are not really dead and that we can talk to them if we want. He has people claiming to do miracles by fooling people with trickery. With others he uses his power to imitate miracles.

This is why God's people must take this important message of warning to the world one last time before Jesus comes. They will be going door-to-door telling everyone that the world is about to end and that God's Word is still true. This message of warning is found in Revelation 14 and is carried by three angels.

Many who have not heard the wonderful message will accept its important truths. They will see and understand parts of God's Word that they did not see before. Some will see the importance of worshipping on His special day for the first time, and now they will discover it to be the test of their loyalty to God as their Creator.

Those who are searching for truth will understand the message and obey it. Because of this they will want to find other people who follow only the Bible so that they can worship God together. This will make many people and leaders angry because they want people to follow them and not God's teachings. It will be very important to know what God's Word says.

We can be thankful that God is fair, and because of this special warning all people will have a chance to know the truth and decide for themselves.

In the end the choice will be clear, and people will understand that to follow Him means eternal life and to follow Satan means death.

Those who honor God's true way will be looked upon as lawbreakers of heaven. Of course this isn't true, but because few at that time will be reading their Bibles, the deception will be very misleading.

Then to make his plan complete, Satan will perform one of his most incredible deceptions. In various places on earth, he will appear as an angel of light sent from heaven. He will perform amazing miracles by healing the sick. Such evidence will be overwhelming for those who do not know the Bible, and Satan's masterful deceptions will be complete.

This message of warning is found in Revelation 14 and is carried by three angels.

Satan will bring terrible times of persecution and destruction upon the world, but God will be with His people. The last great invitation of mercy will go to the world, but unfortunately, it will go at great sacrifice.

What could have been preached during good times will now have to be preached during hard times. Not everyone will agree with what we Christians say. Friends will become our worst enemies. The Bible says that children will betray their parents, and parents will show no mercy to their children who insist on following God's Word. The worst enemies of all will be former Christians who know God's people best. They will turn true believers over to the authorities, and some will even pay with their lives for being true to God.

But God will help His people during these times, and the great promises of the Bible will bring them peace. Those days are fast approaching when all these things will happen, so we must be getting ready now. "Watch therefore, for you do not know what hour your Lord is coming" (Matthew 24:42).

And remember that even though times may be tough, God has given all of us a wonderful promise. "I am with you always, even to the end of the age" (Matthew 28:20).

This means that we will never have to go through tough times alone, because God has told us He will be with us each step of the way.

That is a very important promise. The Bible is full of great promises that will help us through any difficulty that we find ourselves in. But if we are not reading God's Word, we will not know these promises. Then we will have to handle our problems on our own and that never works very well. Jesus loves us and is always there for us. He died on the cross to save us. Now that is one amazing way of saying I will never let you down!

There is another promise that Jesus gave us in His Word to give us great encouragement no matter who we are. So if you're young or old, big or little, you can have confidence if you just remember Philippians 4:13. That promise says, "I can do all things through Christ who strengthens me."

The Bible is full of great promises that will help us through any difficulty.

Our Prayer:

"Dear Jesus, I want to be faithful to You in the difficult times that are coming. Help me to obey Your commandments in the Bible and to tell others the good news of Your soon coming."

Hidden Treasure Questions:

✓ In what different ways is the gospel going to the world today?

✓ What are some of Satan's most incredible deceptions?

Listen to this story online!

Scan for bonus content

Time of Trouble for God's People

This story is taken from *The Great Controversy*, chapter 39, and based on Revelation 22.

Someday soon the gospel work will be finished. When that day comes, the last sermon will have been preached, the last Bible study given, and the last person invited to come to Jesus. The third angel's message will no longer be given, and God's work here on earth will be complete. There will be no more time to plead with people to repent of their sins and receive mercy, because it will be time for the world to end.

In the days of Noah, there came a day when he finally stopped preaching and went into the ark, because it was time for the flood to come.

An angel will return to heaven to announce that God's people have received the latter rain of the Holy Spirit. They have all finished the work that God has given them to do. They have proven themselves loyal to God and His Ten Commandments, and have now received the seal of the living God.

Jesus will then stop His work in the heavenly sanctuary as our Intercessor before God. He will lift His hand and say, "He who is unjust, let him be unjust still; he who is filthy, let him be filthy still; he who is righteous, let him be righteous still; he who is holy, let him be holy still" (Revelation 22:11).

Then He will leave the sanctuary, and darkness will settle over the earth. Everyone will have had a clear chance to decide for or against God's way. All decisions will have been made.

Then the earth will become a very bad place in which to live. The wicked will lose all control and become totally evil because the Holy Spirit will no longer be urging them to do what is right.

Then, as it tells us in chapter 16 of the book of Revelation, there will be seven plagues that will come upon the world, just as they did in Egypt in the time of Moses. The first plague will be one of sores that appear on the wicked.

In the second plague, the sea will turn to blood, and every living creature in it will die.

> They have proven themselves loyal to God and His Ten Commandments, and have now received the seal of the living God.

Then five more plagues will come upon the earth, all punishments for the wicked because of the evil lives they lead. But they will not be sorry for their sins. All during these troubles God's hand will be over His people.

Have you ever noticed how when people are doing something wrong they try to make it sound better by blaming other people who are doing what is right? That is exactly the way it will be then. When all of the problems start happening to the wicked, they will start blaming the people of God for all of the problems. They will become even more angry as they see God watching over those who love Him. In their anger they will want to do everything they can to make God's people miserable. They will even try to get rid of and kill those who are doing right, thinking that this will make them feel better.

The Bible tells the story of Jacob in the Old Testament. When he was young, he tricked his brother out of a blessing that was to be given to the oldest son. For years, his older brother hated him for this. Finally, one day when he was much older, he heard that his brother was coming to meet him. He feared the very worst; surely his brother was coming back to punish him for the wrong that he had done many years before. During the night Jacob wrestled, thinking this might be his last night. His mind began to wonder if God had forgiven him for the wrongs that he had done. Of course God had forgiven him, but Satan was there trying to make him doubt God's goodness and trying to make him give up.

This will be the way it is with God's people. When it looks as if the entire world has turned against them, Satan will come and try to tell them that all is hopeless and that they were far too bad for God to have forgiven them. They will "wrestle in their minds" looking for peace.

But with the story of Jacob, when it started getting light in the morning, he realized that it was not his brother that he was wrestling with. Instead, it was Jesus Himself. Then he began to cling to Jesus and fight to keep his hold on Him instead of fighting to get away. All he wanted now was God's blessing. And so it will be with those who love Jesus during this time of trouble. They may fight with their doubts, but they will come to realize that Jesus is right there with them. Then their greatest desire will be to cling to Him. We can know with assurance that whatever comes to us in the future, God will be there with us. So now is the time to make Jesus your friend and invite Him into your heart. Then in your time of trouble, you can hold on to Him every step of the way.

When people are doing something wrong they try to make it sound better by blaming other people who are doing what is right.

Our Prayer:

"Dear God, help me to know You well so that I can be faithful during the final days of earth's history."

Hidden Treasure Questions:

- ✓ What does Jesus say when He leaves the heavenly sanctuary?
- ✓ How many plagues will come upon the world at the end of time?

Listen to this story online!

Scan for bonus content

Jesus to the Rescue

This story is taken from *The Great Controversy*, chapter 40, and based on Luke 21; Matthew 10:19; Daniel 12:1, 2; Revelation 1, 6, 7, 16; and Jude 24.

The last days of earth's history will be the hardest for God's people. They have been faithful to God and stood for truth, and for this Satan will bring a final time of trouble upon them. Some will flee to the wilderness places to hide in the forests and caves of the mountains. Some will be in prisons awaiting trial by the courts of the land. Some will grow weak from sickness in places where it is a wonder that they have survived at all.

These trials will test God's people as in no other time in history has done. Satan will try his best to discourage Christians, but to no avail. He will tempt them to believe that they have unconfessed sins that will keep them out of heaven and that God cannot save them.

But God will be with His people. He will encourage them through the help of heavenly angels and the Holy Spirit. Angels will visit those in prison who are wondering when Jesus will come to save them from certain death. They will bring God's people words of comfort and in some cases even food.

The people of God will be tempted to feel that God has left them, but they will cling to the promises of the Bible. Their songs of praise will remind them of how God has led them in the past.

Now their time of deliverance will finally come. The wicked will plan to destroy God's people in one day with one final decree, but God will have the last word. As the mobs of evil men rush to attack God's faithful ones, they will be stopped in their tracks by a dense black cloud that surrounds them.

Above God's people is a brilliant rainbow shining with glory from the very throne of God. "Look up!" they will hear a wonderful musical voice say to them. The black angry clouds that were surrounding them will now open like a window, and they will see into the very courtroom of heaven. They will see Jesus on His heavenly throne and hear Him say, "These are my faithful ones. They will soon be with Me to walk among the angels on streets of gold."

It is at the darkest hour that God will deliver His faithful children as He brings His judgments on the world. All nature will seem to be rebelling against the evil people who have taken over the world. The sun will come out to shine at midnight. Stormy clouds will clash overhead. Lightning will jump from the sky, shining from east to west. The shriek of hurricanes will roar all around God's people as huge hailstones destroy the most wicked cities on earth.

The wicked who were so sure that they would destroy God's people will only look on in terror. Demons have controlled them until this day, but now they will realize that their end is near!

The earth will seem to be coming apart. There will be a terrible earthquake as the earth swells and breaks down to its very foundations. Rivers will stop flowing. Mountain chains will come tumbling down. Islands and seaports will disappear into the sea. The homes and buildings of the rich and famous will crumble and collapse. Prison walls will be torn open and God's people set free.

In the middle of all this confusion will be one clear space of indescribable glory from which everyone can hear the voice of God saying, "It is done."

Graves will be opened and many awakened, some to everlasting life and some to eternal death. Those who sacrificed everything to see the gospel go to the world will be in that resurrection. Those who were God's greatest enemies will be there too. The ones who mocked Jesus, spit on Him, and crucified Him will awaken from their graves. Those who persecuted God's people down through the ages and tried to destroy the Bible will be there.

God's children will be filled with peace. Pale, anxious faces will now reflect the wonder, faith, and glory of God. The Father is their refuge and strength.

Then suddenly the clouds will sweep back, revealing the blackness of a star-covered

> **Trials will test God's people as in no other time in history. Satan will try his best to discourage Christians, but to no avail.**

sky. Glorious beams will shine from the open gates of the Holy City. On the open sky will appear a hand holding the two stone tablets of God's commandments folded together. Then the Ten Commandments will be seen traced as with a pen of fire, reminding the wicked of how they have disobeyed His law.

The enemies of God will now see where they were wrong. Ministers of the gospel will realize that they have been fighting against God and have caused countless thousands to be lost. Too late, they will see that the Sabbath of the fourth commandment is the seal of the living God.

The voice of God will then announce the day and hour of Jesus' coming. Like peals of thunder, His voice will roll across the earth. The wicked won't be able to look on the faces of God's people because the glory of heaven will light them up. When heaven's blessing is pronounced on God's people for their loyalty to His holy Sabbath, there will be a mighty shout of victory.

Jesus will call to the sleeping saints. "Wake up! Wake up, all you who sleep in the dust!"

165

Soon there will appear in the east a small black cloud about half the size of a man's hand. This is the cloud that surrounds Jesus and the angels attending Him. The cloud will draw nearer the earth, becoming larger and more glorious with every passing minute. God's people will know that this is the sign of His coming and gaze upon it with thanksgiving.

By now, thousands and thousands of angels will be seen announcing the coming of Jesus with trumpets of praise and judgment! At the very center of the cloud will be Jesus, wrapped in heavenly fire, as King of kings and Lord of lords.

Those who have been His worst enemies will no longer wish to look on Jesus. They will pray to the mountains, calling on the rocks to hide them from His glorious presence! Annas and Caiaphas, the high priests at Jesus' crucifixion, will see Him now as King of kings. The Roman soldiers who beat him and pounded those spikes into His hands will hide their faces from Him. The church leaders who burned millions at the stake will see Him. Too late, they will all realize that they have been at war with God.

Thousands and thousands of angels will be seen.

Now above the roaring of the thunder and flashing of lightning, Jesus will call to the sleeping saints. "Wake up! Wake up, all you who sleep in the dust!" Suddenly millions of faithful ones from every time in history will come from their graves. Those who lived before the flood will be twice as tall as those of us who live today. But all will come out wearing robes of eternal glory, their faces glowing with heaven's light.

The living righteous who have not died will then be changed "in a moment, in the twinkling of an eye." These faithful ones will receive robes of light and the gift of eternal life. Angels will unite families long separated by death, and everyone will be caught up in the air to meet Jesus in the clouds of heaven. What an amazing day that will be!

Our Prayer:

"Dear Jesus, please come into my heart and prepare me for Your soon coming."

Hidden Treasure Questions:

- ✓ What will the earth look like just before Jesus comes?
- ✓ Who will be raised from their graves to see Jesus come again?

Listen to this story online!

Scan for bonus content

Locked up for 1,000 Years

This story is taken from *The Great Controversy*, chapters 41 and 42, and based on Daniel 7; and Revelation 20.

Satan and his evil angels will be left here on earth, after bringing 6,000 years of suffering and death to this world.

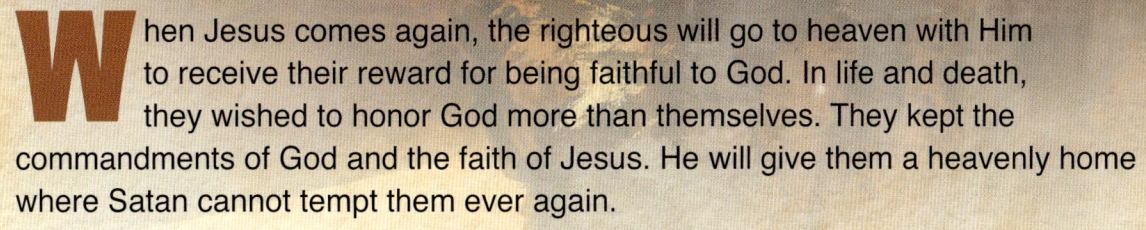

When Jesus comes again, the righteous will go to heaven with Him to receive their reward for being faithful to God. In life and death, they wished to honor God more than themselves. They kept the commandments of God and the faith of Jesus. He will give them a heavenly home where Satan cannot tempt them ever again.

   The wicked cannot go to heaven, and they now realize what they have lost. In despair, they wonder how they could have been so blind to their selfish pride. They were willingly deceived by Satan's temptations because they refused to listen to the voice of God. Now as they see Jesus coming in His glory, they pray for the mountains to fall on them and are destroyed by the brightness of His coming.

   But Satan and his evil angels will be left here on earth. After bringing 6,000 years of suffering and death to this world, they must have time to think about all the trouble they have caused. The Bible tells us that an angel will come down from heaven to lock them up for 1,000 years. This 1,000-year period is called the millennium. When the 1,000 years are finished, Satan will again be released for a little while to tempt the evil nations that will be raised to life.

   Meanwhile, the righteous will be living with Jesus in heaven. They each have been given a home in the Holy City with its streets of gold and gates of pearls. The city has 12 foundations that are made with precious stones, and its walls are made of clear jasper.

   Each child of God will be enjoying all the wonderful things that Jesus has prepared for them. A robe of righteousness has been given to each of them. Those who died as martyrs for Jesus are blessed with a red hem around the bottom of their robes so that everyone will know the sacrifice they have made to honor God's holy name.

   Crowns of gold are put on each person's head, and harps are given to each of them so that they can praise God continually.

   Most important, God's people will get a chance to review the books to see why some are in heaven and others are not. They are sad because some of their loved ones are not with them, but they are so grateful that Jesus died to save them from their sins. Once the 1,000 years are over, the great judgment day must begin. Satan and his angels will be released from their earthly prison to watch as the final events unfold.

Crowns of gold are put on each person's head, and harps are given to each of them.

Jesus and His angels, along with all the redeemed, will descend from heaven. As Christ comes down through the skies, He will call to the wicked dead, and a great resurrection will take place. Billions who have died on earth will come out of their graves looking exactly as they did when they died. They will look very different from the righteous, who were resurrected 1,000 years before. Instead of being clothed with bright robes of glory, they will appear as sick, diseased, and wounded as they did when they went to their graves.

Jesus will return to the place He left 3,000

years before, and as His feet touch the Mount of Olives, it will spread out like a plain. The New Jerusalem in all its dazzling splendor will then come down from heaven and rest on that plain, and Jesus and those who are with Him will go into the city.

Satan will go to gather his forces to fight one last battle against God. He knows he is beaten, but once again, he hopes that he can somehow take over the world. What a mighty army he will have, whose number is as the sand of the sea. There will be mighty giants from the days before the flood and cruel evil rulers who were more monsters than men. There will be great kings, emperors, and military generals who fought terrible battles to control the earth.

Satan will consult with his angels and with the mighty earthly warriors. He will show them that they vastly outnumber the righteous ones inside the city, and together they will plot how they can take the city. Once again, they are blinded by their rage, too foolish to see what can never be. They are facing the God of the universe, and soon He will end evil once and for all.

First, they will march up over the earth's uneven crust now damaged by earthquakes and natural disasters. In the distance, they will see the heavenly city sitting like an island, shimmering in all its glory, and they will fix their gaze on that goal.

As the armies of Satan march up to surround the city, Jesus will order that the gates be closed. Above the city, the wicked will see Jesus sitting on a throne of polished gold. Around His throne are gathered the unnumbered angels and millions of people who have been redeemed. The glory of the Father surrounds them all as it floods the whole earth with His radiance.

Jesus will then be crowned King, and with authority and power, He will announce that the final stage of the judgment must begin.

Daniel saw the whole thing in a vision. He says, "I watched till thrones were put in place, and the Ancient of Days was seated; His garment was white as snow, and the hair of His head was like pure wool. His throne was a fiery flame, its wheels a burning fire; a fiery stream issued and came forth from before Him.

A thousand thousands ministered to Him; ten thousand times ten thousand stood before Him" (Daniel 7:9, 10).

Then the books of heavenly records will be opened, including the Book of Life. Each person will stand before God to receive the reward for the life they have lived. They will see written in the books every deed that they have ever done. Jesus will look into the heart of each evil person there, and all will understand why they have lost the heavenly prize.

Scenes from the entire plan of salvation will be shown across the sky. Everyone will see when Satan first doubted God and turned against his Maker. They will see Adam's temptation and fall in the Garden of Eden, and see how God patiently worked to save His people. They will see the life of Jesus, the Garden of Gethsemane, His cruel trial, and the cross of Calvary.

Satan himself cannot turn from the sight. He will finally admit his mistake in rebelling against God. Satan will kneel to confess that God is merciful, fair, and right to punish the wicked for the evil things they have done.

Then it will be over. There will be nothing else for God to do but to bring fire down upon all the wicked. This is the second death. Anyone not found written in the book of life will be cast into the lake of fire, and they will be burned up.

> **Satan will consult with his angels and with the mighty earthly warriors.**

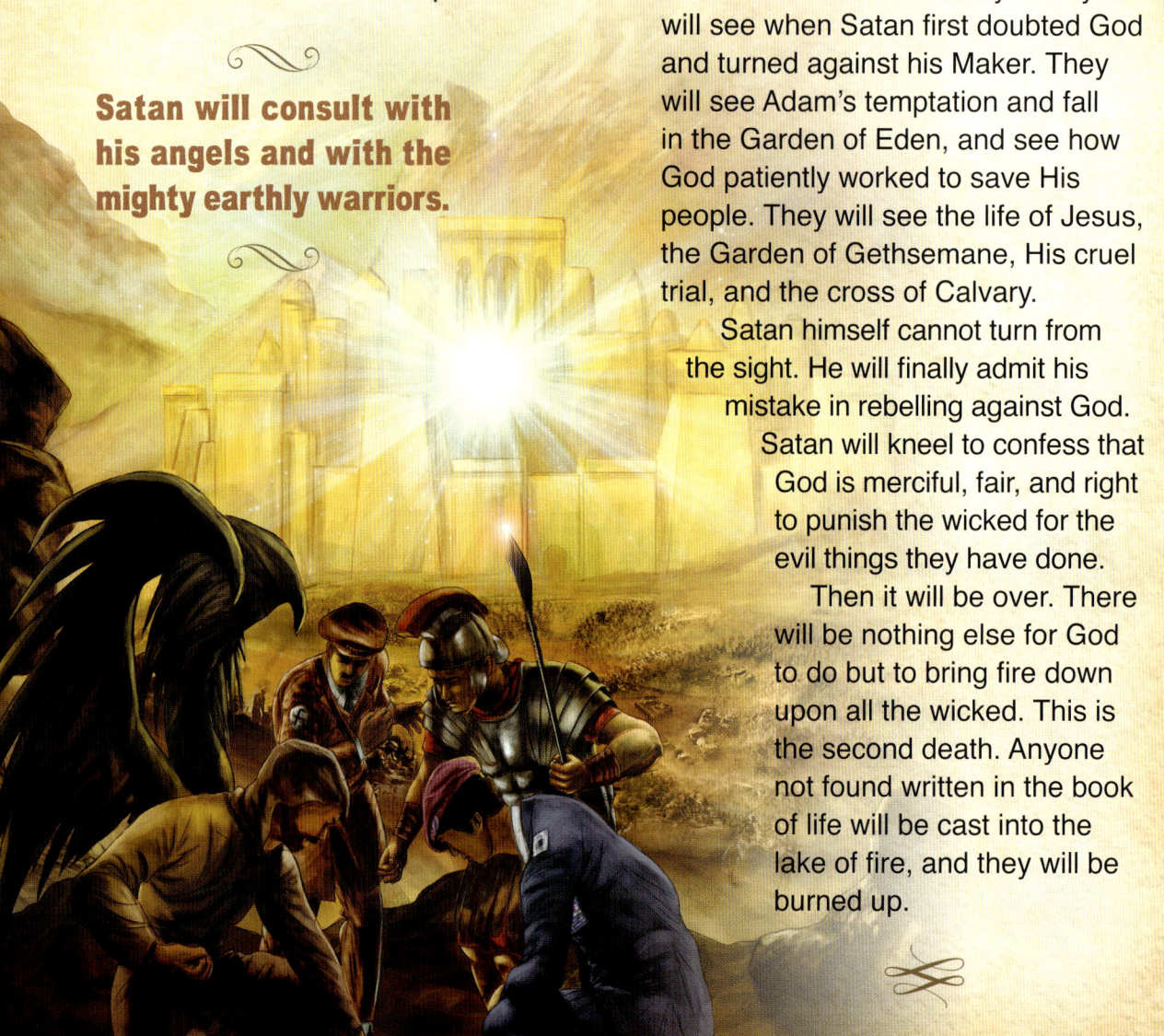

Our Prayer:

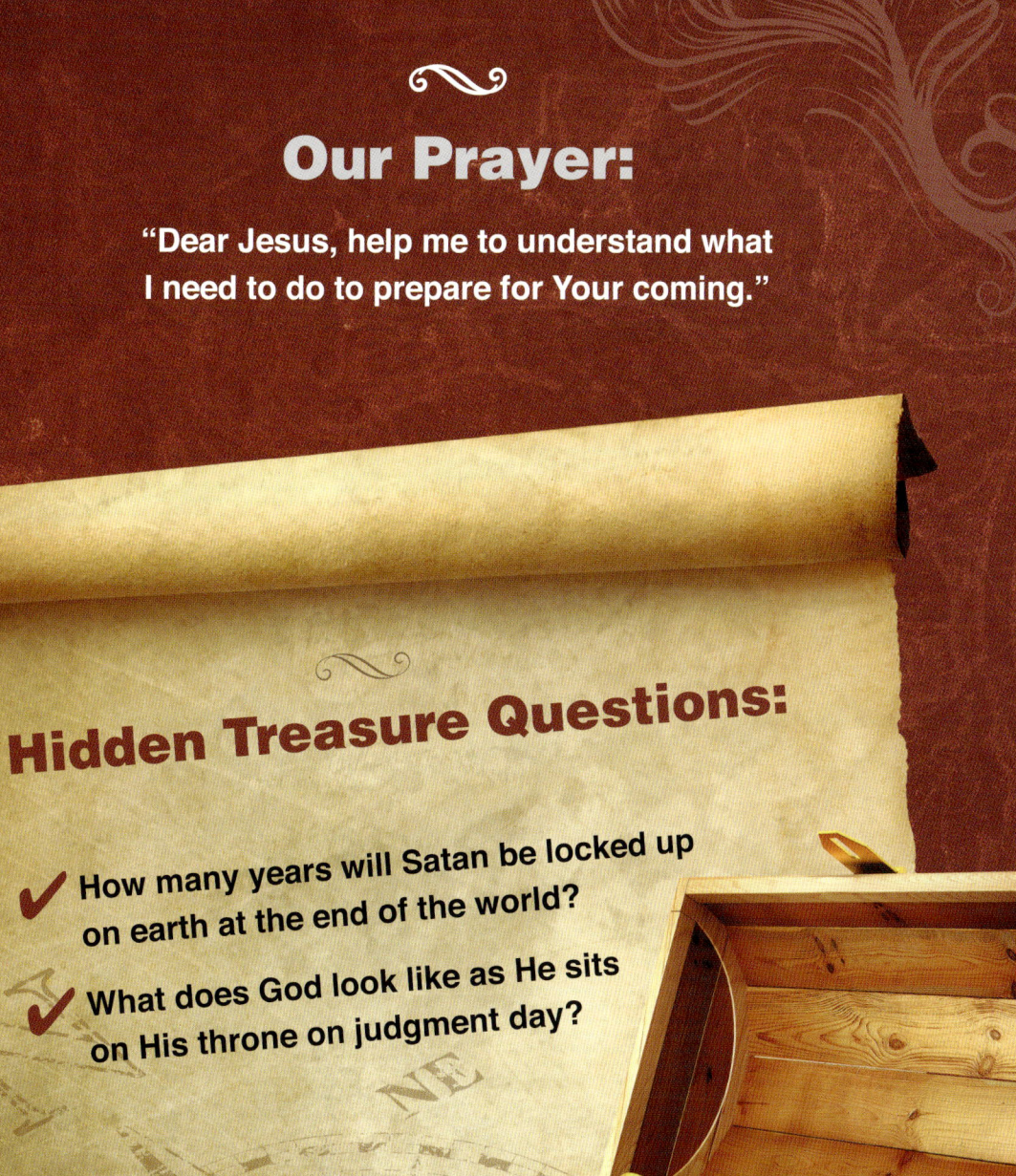

"Dear Jesus, help me to understand what I need to do to prepare for Your coming."

Hidden Treasure Questions:

✓ How many years will Satan be locked up on earth at the end of the world?

✓ What does God look like as He sits on His throne on judgment day?

Listen to this story online!

Scan for bonus content

God's Perfect Playground

This story is taken from *The Great Controversy*, chapter 42, and based on Revelation 21 and 22.

The war between good and evil is over. Judgment day has come and gone. Satan and his evil demons have been destroyed in the lake of fire. There is nothing but quiet across the face of the earth.

Now God makes a new planet to replace the one destroyed by Satan. Millions of God's creatures gather to watch. Men and women, boys and girls, angels and beings from every corner of space marvel at this new beginning.

What will that new world be like? It will be more beautiful than we can ever imagine, because God has promised that Eden will one day be restored. What is really exciting is that we will get to see it all happen before our very eyes.

There will be hills and valleys with every kind of tree and flower possible. There will be grapevines and oak trees in the forests, mango trees and coconut palms on the beaches, and flowers of every color scattered across the hills and plains.

> **Now God makes a new planet to replace the one destroyed by Satan. Millions of God's creatures gather to watch.**

Animals, birds, and insects will be everywhere. They will be all sizes and shapes, just as they were created in Eden so long ago. We will see lions and lambs, ostriches and owls, and beetles and bees. Frogs and fish will fill the streams, and whales and dolphins will play in the sea.

The new world will be so big that there will be enough space for each of us to have a home of our own in the country. We will build our homes however we want them, wherever we want them, and with whatever materials we want to use. Some people will build their home with gold, silver, or jewels, or some with marble or whatever else God may provide.

We will never again have to work as hard as we do now. We will never again have blisters on our hands, backaches, or thorns pricking our fingers when we pick the roses in our gardens.

There will be no more death, crying, or pain, for the curse of sin will be gone. Leaves will no longer fall from the trees, and flowers will never fade or wilt when we pick them.

Little children will run and play with animals that they could never play with on earth. Lions and bears will be our friends when that day comes.

The Holy City will be here with its streets of gold, and each of the 12 gates will be a huge, shining pearl. We will have country homes and mansions in the city, too. The throne of God will be the center of the city. This planet will then become the center of the universe. Glorious beings will come from far and wide to worship God and to hear the story of salvation. In the city there will be no need for the sun, because God will be its light by day, and there will be no more night.

We will learn new things every day, for God is the source of all knowledge. We will understand music, architecture, history, and mathematics in that heavenly city. The treasures of the universe will be open to our minds as we study the subjects of astronomy, biology, and anatomy.

But the favorite subject of all will be the science of salvation. How did God ever make a plan that would bring an end to sin and yet offer salvation to the sinners who wanted it?

Our minds will forever be searching for the answers to that question. Through the endless ages, we will continue to grow in grace and intelligence because God our Father is the source of light, life, and love in the universe. This has all been made possible because He sent His only Son to die for us, "that whoever believes in Him should not perish but have everlasting life" (John 3:16).

That is the story of the great controversy between good and evil. Sin and sinners are no more. The entire universe is clean. One pulse of harmony and gladness beats throughout the vast creation. From the Creator of all things flow life, light, and gladness throughout the vast reaches of space. From the tiniest atom to the greatest world, all things in their beauty and perfect joy declare that "God is love."

I can't wait to be there. How about you?

The Holy City will be here with its streets of gold, and each of the 12 gates will be a huge, shining pearl.

Our Prayer:

"Dear Heavenly Father, I can't wait until You create the new earth. What an exciting day that will be!"

Hidden Treasure Questions:

✓ What subjects will we study in the new world to come?

✓ Why will we not need the light of the sun in the new earth?

Listen to this story online!

Scan for bonus content

Title Index

TITLE	BOOK	PAGE
The Fallen Angel	1	4
Let There Be Light	1	8
God Creates the Animals	1	12
In the Image of God	1	16
The First Sabbath	1	20
The Fall of Adam and Eve	1	24
God's Wonderful Plans for Adam and Eve	1	30
Cain and Abel	1	34
Noah's Ark	1	38
The Flood	1	44
Tower of Babel	1	50
Job	1	54
Call of Abram	1	60
Sodom and Gomorrah	1	64
The Test of Faith	1	70
A Wife for Isaac	1	76
Jacob and Esau	1	82
Jacob's Ladder	1	88
Night of Wrestling	1	92
Joseph's Coat and Dreams	1	98
Joseph in Egypt	1	104
Joseph and His Brothers	1	110
Moses	1	116
Let My People Go	1	122
The Passover	1	128
Crossing the Red Sea	1	132
Ten Commandments	1	136

TITLE	BOOK	PAGE
Idolatry at Sinai	1	140
Tabernacle and Its Services	1	144
Sin of Nadab and Abihu	1	150
Food From Heaven Rejected (God's People Complain About Manna)	1	154
Twelve Spies	1	158
Rebellion of Korah	1	164
Moses Makes a Big Mistake (Moses Strikes the Rock Twice)	1	170
Fiery Snakes (Children of Israel Bitten by Snakes)	1	176
Great Victory Over Sihon and Og	1	180
Balaam and His Talking Donkey	1	184
The River Stopped Running (Crossing the Jordan)	1	188
Fall of Jericho	2	4
Achan's Deception	2	10
Tricked by the Gibeonites	2	14
The Day the Sun Stood Still	2	18
The Earlier Judges	2	22
God Chooses Gideon	2	28
Gideon's Army	2	34
Victory Over the Midianites	2	38
Ruth	2	42
Samson	2	48
Samson Gets Even	2	54
Samson and Delilah	2	60
A Mother's Prayer Answered (Hannah's Prayer)	2	66

TITLE	BOOK	PAGE
God Calls Samuel	2	70
The Ark of God Taken	2	76
We Want a King! (Saul is Made King)	2	82
Saul's Sacrifice	2	86
Saul Rejected as King	2	90
Jonathan Wins the Battle	2	94
David Anointed King	2	98
David Kills the Lion	2	104
David Brought Before the King	2	108
David and Goliath	2	112
King Saul is Jealous of David	2	118
Doeg's Betrayal	2	124
Saul Chases David	2	128
David Shows Kindness to Saul	2	132
Abigail	2	136
David Steals Saul's Spear	2	142
Witch of Endor	2	146
David With the Philistines	2	152
David Crowned King	2	156
The Philistines Defeated	2	160
David and Mephiboseth	2	164
David and Bathsheba	2	168
Absalom	2	172
Absalom Rebels	2	176
Absalom Killed	2	182
David Chooses Solomon as King	2	188
God Gives Solomon Wisdom	3	4
Wise King, Foolish Mistake	3	8
The Kingdom Divided	3	14
A Kingdom Turns From God	3	18

TITLE	BOOK	PAGE
Elijah Predicts a Drought	3	22
Miracle in a Jar (God Provides for a Widow)	3	28
Elijah Raises a Boy to Life	3	34
Mount Carmel Showdown (Elijah Calls Down Fire)	3	40
Elijah Flees to Mount Horeb	3	46
The Call of Elisha	3	50
A Wicked King Becomes a Thief (King Ahab Steals from Naboth)	3	54
Elijah and Horses of Fire	3	58
Elisha Heals the Water at Jericho	3	62
Elisha and the Bears	3	66
Ditches of Blood (Moabites See Ditches of Blood)	3	70
The Miracle Oil Pots	3	74
Resurrected Boy at Shunem	3	80
Healing Naaman	3	84
The Floating Ax Head	3	90
Delivery at Dothan	3	96
Jonah and the Whale	3	100
A Boy Becomes King	3	106
Hezekiah's Reformation	3	110
Hezekiah's Deliverance From Assyria	3	114
Hezekiah's Sickness	3	120
Josiah's Reformation	3	124
Jeremiah, A Man for His Time	3	128
Jerusalem Captured	3	132
In the Babylonian Court	3	136
Nebuchadnezzar's Dream	3	142
The Fiery Furnace	3	146
Nebuchadnezzar's Madness	3	152

TITLE	BOOK	PAGE
Handwriting on the Wall	3	156
In the Lions' Den	3	162
Return of the Exiles	3	168
Beauty Queen	3	172
A Courageous Queen Saves Her People	3	178
Nehemiah Rebuilds Jerusalem	3	184
The Coming Deliverer	3	188
The Mother of Jesus is Chosen	4	4
The Birth of Jesus	4	8
The Dedication of Jesus	4	14
Wise Men	4	18
Jesus in the Temple	4	24
The Boy Jesus	4	30
John the Baptist	4	34
Baptism of Jesus	4	38
Wilderness Temptation	4	42
We Have Found the Messiah	4	48
Jesus' First Miracle	4	52
Jesus Clears the Temple	4	56
Nicodemus	4	62
Woman at the Well	4	66
Healing the Nobleman's Son	4	72
Healing a Lame Man at Bethesda	4	76
Hidden Treasure	4	82
Death of John the Baptist	4	86
Jesus Rejected at Nazareth	4	92
Miracle Fish (Disciples Receive a Miracle)	4	96
A Demon in the Church (Jesus Healed a Man in Church)	4	100
A Leper Comes to Jesus	4	104

TITLE	BOOK	PAGE
Miracles at Peter's House	4	108
Paralytic Healed	4	112
Matthew Gets a New Job	4	118
Your Disciples Broke the Rules (Disciples Picked Grain on the Sabbath)	4	122
Twelve Special Men Chosen	4	126
Sermon on the Mount	4	130
The Foolish Carpenter	4	136
Centurion's Request	4	140
Widow's Son Raised	4	146
The Farmer's Seed (Parable of the Sower)	4	152
Calming the Storm	4	156
Demons on the Beach (Jesus Confronts Two Wild Men)	4	162
Healed by a Touch	4	166
Jairus' Daughter Raised	4	170
Only One Gave Thanks	4	176
The First Evangelists	4	180
Look What I Have	4	184
The Great Supper	4	188
The Son Who Left His Father (Prodigal Son)	5	4
A Small Lunch and 5,000 Hungry People	5	10
Peter Walks on Water	5	16
A Mother's Great Faith Saves Her Daughter	5	22
An Unforgettable Night	5	26
Demon-Possessed Boy	5	30
Money in a Fish's Mouth	5	34
Blind Man Healed	5	38
The Lost Sheep	5	44

TITLE	BOOK	PAGE
Good Samaritan	5	48
Rich Young Ruler	5	54
At the Home of Lazarus	5	60
A Lesson on True Greatness (Jesus Teaches Humility)	5	64
"Lazarus, Come Forth!"	5	68
Church Leaders Plan a Murder (Pharisees Decide Jesus Must Die)	5	74
Two Prayers, One Answer	5	78
Zacchaeus	5	84
The Best Gift Jesus Ever Received	5	88
The Unforgiving Servant	5	94
Jesus' Triumphal Entry	5	98
A Den of Thieves	5	104
The Stolen Vineyard	5	110
Sheep and Goats	5	114
Look for My Return	5	118
The Hidden Money	5	124
Ten Maidens	5	128
First Communion	5	132
A Terrible Night in the Garden	5	136
Judas Betrays Jesus	5	142
Trial Before Annas and Caiaphas	5	146
The Man Who Hung Himself (Judas Ends His Life)	5	150
In Pilate's Judgment Hall	5	154
Crucify Him	5	158
Calvary	5	162
In Joseph's Tomb	5	168
Jesus' Resurrection	5	172
An Empty Tomb	5	178

TITLE	BOOK	PAGE
The Walk to Emmaus	5	182
Feed My Sheep (God Instructs Peter)	5	186
God's Purpose for His Church (The Gospel Continues)	6	4
Preaching With New Power	6	10
Miracle at the Gate (Peter Heals a Cripple)	6	14
Peter and John in Trouble Again (Peter and John Arrested)	6	18
Ananias and Sapphira	6	24
Peter and John Imprisoned	6	30
The Stoning of Stephen	6	34
Philip and the Ethiopian	6	40
Simon the Sorcerer	6	44
From Persecutor to Preacher (Saul - A Changed Man)	6	48
Dorcas Raised to Life	6	54
Peter and the Sheet	6	58
Chained Between Two Soldiers	6	64
Adventures in Antioch	6	70
An Angry Mob Stones Paul	6	74
Fighting in Church (Disciples Settle an Argument)	6	80
Timothy Joins Paul	6	84
Earthquake at Midnight	6	88
They've Turned the World Upside Down! (Paul and Silas in Thessalonica)	6	94
Who Is the Unknown God?	6	98
Paul at Corinth	6	104
Healed by a Handkerchief (Paul Heals in Amazing Ways)	6	108
Success and Danger in Ephesus	6	112

TITLE	BOOK	PAGE
A Young Man Falls to His Death (A Boy Falls Out a Window)	6	118
Saved by the Romans	6	122
Paul Before the Sanhedrin	6	128
A King Almost Becomes a Christian (Paul Impresses King Agrippa)	6	132
Shipwrecked! (Paul Is Caught in a Violent Storm)	6	138
Paul Is Bitten by a Deadly Snake	6	142
Special Armor for God's Special Forces	6	146
Paul Helps a Runaway Slave	6	150
Spreading the Gospel From Prison	6	154
I Have Fought the Good Fight	6	158
Peter Is Faithful to the End	6	164
John Is Boiled in Oil	6	168
Seven Messages From Seven Churches	6	172
A Woman and a Child Hunted by a Dragon (Revelation Describes the Church)	6	178
John Receives a Heavenly Vision	6	182
God Leads His Church to Success	6	186
Jerusalem Will Be Destroyed	7	4
Satan Tries to Stamp Out the Christian Church	7	10
Church of the Dark Ages	7	16
The Waldenses	7	22
John Wycliffe	7	28
Huss and Jerome	7	32
Martin Luther as a Young Man	7	36
Martin and the Scary Staircase	7	40
Martin Luther Goes to Court	7	44
Revival in Switzerland	7	48
The French Reformation	7	52

TITLE	BOOK	PAGE
Bow or Burn at the Stake	7	58
Tyndale the Translator	7	62
John Bunyan Jailed	7	68
Christians Flee to America	7	72
Roger Williams	7	76
Saved From a Fire	7	80
Two Brothers Dedicated to God	7	84
God Is Banned in France	7	88
Bloody Moon and Falling Stars	7	92
A Little Boy Makes a Big Decision	7	98
William Miller	7	102
God Chooses a Simple Farmer	7	106
Great Disappointment	7	110
God Gives a Long Look Into the Future	7	114
God's Special Day	7	118
What's Going on in the Courts of Heaven?	7	122
The Greatest Battle	7	126
Satan's Deadly Tricks	7	132
What Happens When We Die?	7	136
A Storm Is Coming	7	140
The Amazing Word of God	7	146
The Final Warning	7	152
Time of Trouble for God's People	7	158
Jesus to the Rescue	7	162
Locked up for 1,000 Years	7	168
God's Perfect Playground	7	174
Title Index	7	178
Topical Index	7	183
Men and Women of the Bible	7	186

Topical Index

TOPIC	BOOK	PAGE
Acceptance	5	8
Accepting Others	5	86
Angels	1	4, 88
	4	5, 11, 35
	6	64
	7	152
Anger	1	36, 174
Anger, Danger of	1	36
Armor of God	6	147
Baptism	4	38
Baptism	6	42, 44, 62
Belief	5	31
Bible, God's Protection of	7	146
Bible Study	4	84, 154
	6	99
Bible, Trust in	3	142
Born Again	4	63
Bravery	2	104, 114
Cheerfulness	6	90
Choices	1	68
	2	42
Choosing Jesus	5	58
Clean heart	4	116
Complaining	1	155
Confession	3	12
Conversion	4	63, 120
Courage	3	146, 162
	6	21

TOPIC	BOOK	PAGE
Coveting	2	12
	3	54
Creation	1	8
Death	2	149
	7	136
Deception	1	86
Deliverance	3	114
Disobedience	1	151
Dreams	1	88
	2	34
	3	142
	6	58
Eating Right, Results of	1	155
End of Sin	1	32
Eternal Life	4	64
Example	5	92
Faith	3	88
	4	168
	5	24
Faithful, Being	1	161
Faithfulness	5	31
Faithfulness Till Death	6	161
Faithfulness to God	5	126
Fear	3	175
First Wedding	4	52
Forgiveness	4	115
	5	8, 94
Friendship	5	60

TOPIC	BOOK	PAGE
Friends, Influence of	2	166
God's Leading	3	84
God's Word	1	138
Gratitude	4	120
Greed	4	186
Heaven	6	166
	7	168, 174
Help	1	178
	6	179
Helping Needy	3	36, 38
Helping Others	6	55
Help in Trouble	3	25, 32, 74, 94
	4	160
Holy Spirit	5	128
	7	10, 14, 152
Honesty	6	25
Humility	2	140
Idols	1	141
	3	126
	6	100
Jealousy	1	102
	2	119
	3	163
Keeping Eyes on God	1	58
	3	118
Kindness	1	114
	2	132, 140, 166
	5	52, 61
	6	86, 96
Listen to God	1	126
	5	116

TOPIC	BOOK	PAGE
Listening to God	6	70, 71
Looking at the Real Person	5	78
Lying	2	126
	6	28
Martyr	6	38
Miracles	1	122, 132, 188
	2	18, 66
	3	28, 34, 62, 74, 80, 90, 120, 146, 162,
	4	52, 72, 96, 100, 104, 108, 112, 140, 146, 156, 170
	5	10, 16, 34, 38, 68, 172
	6	14, 54, 108
Missionaries	4	180
Mother	5	23
Mother, Faith of	2	68
New Birth	4	63
Obedience	1	74
	4	32
Obedience, Importance of	1	61
	3	86, 88, 104
Obedience, Respect for	3	104
Obedience to Parents	2	52
Passover	1	128
	4	24
	5	104, 132
Patience	5	4
Pentecost	6	10
Plagues	1	122

TOPIC	BOOK	PAGE
	7	158
Power Over Devil	6	10
Praise	3	82
Prayer	3	43
	5	81
Prayer, Answer to	2	66, 67
	3	80
Prayer, Faithfulness in	3	164
Pride	1	128
Priorities	5	62
Promise of a Redeemer	6	8, 184
Promises, Keeping	6	25
Prophecy	3	144
Protection	3	146, 162
	4	160
	6	142, 144
Rebellion	1	165
	2	182
	3	132
Respect	2	132, 144
	3	68
Resurrection	3	80
	5	72, 174
	6	56, 96
Resurrection, Final	7	170
Reverence	1	150
Robe of Righteousness	7	42
Rudeness	2	139
Running from God	3	100
Sabbath	1	20, 154
	7	13, 118

TOPIC	BOOK	PAGE
Salvation	5	121
Salvation, Do Not Put Off	6	136
Second Coming	5	121, 190
	7	165
Selfishness	4	186
Service	5	58
Sharing	5	12
Signs of Jesus Coming	5	118
	7	92
Sin, Origin of	7	132
Sin, Results of	1	6
	5	126
Temple	1	145
Temptation	2	10
	6	147, 148
Ten Commandments	1	136, 140
Test of Faith	7	130
Thankfulness	4	178
Trials	1	41, 58
	5	66
	6	92
True Greatness	2	112
Trusting God	1	74
	4	160
Unselfishness	2	139, 140
Wisdom	3	4, 5
Witnessing	4	132
	6	101, 108
Witnessing when Persecuted	6	156
Worship	3	146
Worship, Freedom to	7	78

Men and Women of the Bible

TOPIC	BOOK
Aaron	**1**: 123, 126, F130, 140, 146, 150-152, 165, 166, 171-174, 176; **4**: 34
Abagail	**2**: 136, 139, 140
Abednego (Azariah)	**3**: 133, 137, 140, 146-150; **6**: 7
Abel	**1**: 34-36
Abiathar	**2**: 126, 128, 129, 176-178, 185, 188, 190
Abiham	**3**: 18, 19
Abihu	**1**: 150-152
Abinadab (son of Jesse)	**2**: 99
Abiram	**1**: 165-167
Abishai	**2**: 142, 143, 158, 180, 185
Abner	**2**: 119, 142, 144, 156-158
Abraham	**1**: 65, 66, 70-74, 76-80, 88, 104, 108, 118, 184, 189; **3**: 43, 111, 172, 188; **4**: 39, 44; **5**: 86; **6**: 5, 15, 37, 80; **7**: 129
Absalom	**2**: 172-174, 176, 177, 179-180, 182-186, 188
Achan	**2**: 10-12
Achish	**2**: 146, 147
Adam	**1**: 16-18, 20-22, 26-32, 34; **3**: 188; **4**: 4, 43, 44; **6**: 4, 178; **7**: 118, 122, 126-128, 140, 172
Adonijah	**2**: 188-190
Agag	**2**: 90, 91
Agrippa	**6**: 64, 134-136
Ahab	**3**: 20, 22, 24, 25, 28, 41, 42, 47, 54-56; **6**: 7
Ahasuerus	**3**: 172, 174, 179, 181, 182
Ahaz (king of Judah)	**3**: 110
Ahaziah (king of Isreal)	**3**: 56
Ahaziah (king of Judah)	**3**: 106
Ahijah	**3**: 14, 19
Ahimaaz	**2**: 178, 179, 184, 185
Ahimelech	**2**: 126
Aholiab	**1**: 147
Alden, John	**7**: 74
Alexander	**6**: 115

TOPIC	BOOK
Alexander (the Great)	**3**: 143
Amalekites	**2**: 29, 32, 90-92, 147, 148
Amnon	**2**: 172
Amram	**1**: 117
Ananias (from Damascus)	**6**: 51, 125
Ananias (high Priest)	**6**: 128, 132
Ananias (husband of Sapphira)	**6**: 24-27
Andrew	**4**: 49, 50, 96, 98, 118, 126; **5**: 12-14, 119
Anna	**4**: 16
Annas	**5**: 146; **7**: 165
Aquila	**6**: 104
Artaxerxes	**3**: 169, 184; **7**: 115
Asa	**3**: 19, 20
Asahel	**2**: 156, 158
Asher	**2**: 32, 39; **3**: 111
Ashpenaz	**3**: 137, 138, 140
Athaliah (queen of Judah)	**3**: 106, 107
Azariah	**3**: 133, 137, 140
Baasha	**3**: 19, 20
Balaam	**1**: 184-186; **3**: 172
Balak	**1**: 184, 185
Barabbas	**5**: 158, 159
Barak	**2**: 26
Barnabas	**6**: 25, 52, 71, 72, 75-78, 80, 81, 84, 85
Baruch	**3**: 134
Bathsheba	**2**: 168, 169, 189
Belshazzar	**3**: 156-159
Belteshazzar (Daniel)	**3**: 137
Benaiah	**2**: 188-190
Benjamin	**1**: 99, 112-114
Benjamin (tribe of)	**2**: 83, 84; **3**: 15
Bereans	**6**: 100

TOPIC	BOOK
Bernice	**6**: 135
Berquin, Louis	**7**: 52, 54-56, 88
Bethuel	**1**: 78, 79
Bishop of Durham	**7**: 65
Boaz	**2**: 45, 46
Bradford, William	**7**: 74
Bunyan, John	**7**: 68-70
Caesar	**5**: 154, 156, 159; **6**: 95, 135, 155
Caesar (Augustus)	**4**: 8
Caesar (Tiberius)	**4** :38
Caiaphas	**5**: 75, 76, 146; **7**: 165
Cain	**1**: 34-36; **6**: 4
Caleb	**1**: 159-162; **2**: 25
Calvin, John	**7**: 55, 56, 88
Cestius	**7**: 6
Charles V	**7**: 45, 58, 59
Chilion	**2**: 42
Cleopas	**5**: 182-184, 189
Constantine	**7**: 13, 14, 16, 17
Cornelius	**6**: 60-62, 70, 71
Cromwell, Thomas	**7**: 66
Cyrus	**3**: 143, 157, 160, 168
Dan (tribe of)	**2**: 49
Daniel	**3**: 128, 137-140, 142-144, 152, 153, 158-160, 163-166, 172; **6**:7, 184; **7**: 95, 103, 104, 107, 112, 149, 171
Darius (king of Persia)	**3**: 169
Darius (the Mede)	**3**: 160, 163
Dathan	**1**: 165-167
David	**2**: 46, 98, 100-102, 104-106, 108-110, 112-116, 118-122, 124-126, 128-130, 132-134, 136-140, 142-144, 146, 147, 149, 152-154, 156-158, 160-162, 164-166, 168-170, 172, 173, 176-180, 182, 183, 185, 186, 188-190; **3**: 4, 6, 11, 16, 18, 110, 120, 124, 125, 189; **4**: 5, 6, 122; **5**: 23, 99, 100, 105, 107; **6**: 7; **7**: 5, 90
Deborah	**2**: 24-26
Delilah	**2**: 60, 62
Demetrius	**6**: 113-115
Diocletian	**7**: 13

TOPIC	BOOK
Doeg	**2**: 124, 126
Dorcas	**6**: 54-56
Drusilla	**6**: 134
Ebed-Melech	**3**: 129
Eck	**7**: 49, 50
Edson, Hiram	**7**: 111, 112
Eglon	**2**: 19, 22, 25
Ehud	**2**: 22, 25
Elah	**2**: 106; **3**: 19, 20
Eleazar (Aaron's son)	**2**: 126, 127
Eli	**2**: 67, 68, 70-74, 77, 78
Eliab	**2**: 99, 112
Eliakim	**3**: 116, 117
Eliezer	**1**: 76-80; **2**: 42
Elijah	**3**: 20-22, 24-26, 28-32, 34-38, 41-44, 46-48, 50-52, 55, 56, 58-60, 62-64, 66, 68; **4**: 34, 38, 90, 93; **5**: 27, 28, 35, 165; **6**: 7; **7**: 143, 147, 149, 165
Elisha	**3**: 50-52, 58-60, 62-64, 66-68, 70, 71, 74, 76-78, 80-82, 84-86, 88, 90-93, 96-98; **4**: 93, 105; **7**: 137
Elizabeth	**4**: 34-36
Elkanah	**2**: 66
Elymas	**6**: 72
Enoch	**3**:188
Ephraim (tribe of)	**1**: 159; **2**: 24, 25, 39, 40, 66, 186; **3**: 111, 112, 126
Esau	**1**: 82-86, 94-96, 99, 176
Esther	**3**: 172-179, 181, 182; **6**: 7
Eutychus	**6**: 119, 120
Eve	**1**: 19-22, 24, 26, 34, 38; **3**: 188; **4**: 4, 43; **6**: 4, 178; **7**: 118, 122, 126-128, 137
Ezra	**3**: 169, 170, 184; **6**: 7
Felix	**6**: 132-136
Festus	**6**: 134-136
Gabriel	**4**: 5, 11, 34, 35
Gallio	**6**: 106
Gamaliel	**6**: 32, 33, 126
Gehazi	**3**: 81, 82
Geshem	**3**: 185

TOPIC	BOOK
Gideon	**2**: 28-32, 34-36, 38-40; **6**: 6
Goliath	**2**: 112-116, 118, 124, 125, 165
Gregory VII	**7**: 20
Gutenberg, Johann	**7**: 147, 149
Hadad	**3**: 12
Hadassah	**3**: 172, 174
Haggai	**3**: 169
Haman	**3**: 174, 175, 178-182
Hananiah (Shadrach)	**3**: 133, 137, 140
Hannah	**2**: 66-68, 72
Hazael	**3**: 51
Hegai	**3**: 172
Henry IV	**7**: 19
Henry VIII	**7**: 65
Herod, King	**4**: 20-23, 27, 30, 34
Herod Agrippa	**6**: 64, 65, 67
Herod Antipas	**4**: 87-90; **5**: 84, 112, 155, 156; **7**: 11
Hezekiah	**3**: 110-112, 114-118, 120-122, 132; **6**:7
Hilkiah	**3**: 125, 126
Hiram	**2**: 161, 162; **3**: 6, 8
Hophni	**2**: 67, 71-73, 77
Huldah	**3**: 126
Hushai	**2**: 179, 183-185
Huss, John	**7**: 30, 32-34, 48
Isaac	**1**: 70-73, 76, 77, 80-82, 84, 85, 88, 108, 118, 184, 189; **3**: 43, 111, 188; **4**: 44; **6**: 15
Isaiah	**3**: 118, 120-122, 132, 168; **4**: 26, 49, 92; **5**: 168; **6**: 7, 40
Ishbosheth	**2**: 156, 157, 165
Jabin	**2**: 24-26
Jacob	**1**: 82-86, 88-90, 92-96, 98-100, 102, 104, 108, 111-113, 118, 176, 184, 189; **3**: 188; **4**: 18, 67; **6**: 5, 15
Jael	**2**: 26
Jahaziel	**3**: 71
Jairus	**4**: 170-174; **7**: 143
James (son of Alphaeus)	**4**: 127

TOPIC	BOOK
James (brother of John)	**4**: 49, 96, 98, 118, 126, 173, 181; **5**: 26, 30, 65, 66, 119, 138, 187, 189; **6**: 64, 82, 160; **7**: 11
Jason	**6**: 94, 95
Jehoahaz	**3**: 132
Jehoiachin	**3**: 133
Jehoiada	**3**: 106-108
Jehoiakim	**3**: 128, 133, 137
Jehoram	**3**: 70
Jehoshaphat	**3**: 70-72
Jehu	**3**: 51, 56
Jeremiah	**3**: 128-130, 134; **5**: 35; **6**: 7
Jeroboam	**3**: 12, 14-16, 19
Jerome	**7**: 32, 34
Jesse	**2**: 99, 101, 108, 110
Jesus	**1**:4-6, 8, 16, 35, 66, 68, 73, 128, 130, 133, 138, 142, 156, 173, 174, 178, 186; **2**:15, **3**:12, 37, 38, 100, 144, 189, 190; **4**: 4,5,8, 10-12, 14-16, 18, 20-22, 24-28, 30-32, 35, 36, 38-40, 42-46, 48-50, 52-54, 56-60, 62-64, 66-70, 72-74, 76-80, 82-84, 87, 89, 92-94, 96-98, 100-102, 104-106, 108-110, 112-116, 118-120, 122-124, 126-128, 130-134, 136-138, 140-144, 146-150, 152-154, 157-160, 163-164, 166, 168, 170, 172-174, 176, 178, 180, 182, 184, 186, 188, 190, 191; **5**: 7, 11-14, 16-20, 22-24, 26-28, 30-32, 34, 36, 38, 30-32, 34-36, 39-42, 44-46, 49, 51, 52, 54-58, 60-62, 64-66, 68-72, 74-76, 78, 79, 82, 85, 86, 88-92, 94, 95, 98-102, 105-108, 110-112, 114-116, 119-122, 124, 126, 128, 130, 132-134, 137-140, 142-144, 146-148, 150-152, 154-156, 158-160, 163-166, 168-170, 172, 174-176, 178-180, 182-184, 186-190; **6**: 4, 7, 8, 10, 12, 15, 16, 19-22, 24, 28, 31, 32, 34-36, 40-42, 44-45, 48, 50-52, 54-56, 59, 61, 64, 70, 71, 75-78. 80-81, 88-92, 95, 96, 99-102, 104, 105, 109-110, 112, 113, 118, 119, 123, 128, 129, 135, 143, 148, 152, 155, 156, 161, 162 164-166, 168-170, 172-176, 178, 180, 184, 186, 187, 189, 190; **7**: 5-8, 10-14, 16, 23, 26, 32, 34, 37, 40, 42, 44, 48-50, 52-56, 59, 65, 66, 68-70, 81, 82, 86, 89, 92-96, 98-100, 102-104, 106-108, 110-112, 115, 116, 120, 122-124, 126-130, 132, 134, 136-138, 140-141, 144, 150, 153, 154, 156, 158-160, 162-166, 169-172

TOPIC	BOOK
Jezebel	**3**: 20, 22, 24, 40, 47, 50, 54, 56, 66
Joab	**2**: 156-158, 161, 169, 173, 185, 188, 190
Joah	**3**: 116, 117
Joash	**3**: 106-108
Job	**1**: 54-58
Jochebed	**1**: 117, 118
Joel	**6**: 12
John (the apostle)	**4**: 49, 50, 96, 98, 118, 126, 149, 173; **5**: 26, 30, 65, 66, 119, 132, 138, 165, 179, 187; **6**: 14-16, 18-21, 30-32, 46, 64, 168, 169, 170, 172, 178-180, 182, 186; **7**: 11, 13
John (the Baptist)	**4**: 34-36, 38-40, 42, 48-50, 66, 87-90, 126; **5**: 112; **6**: 109, 168
John Mark	**6**: 67, 72, 84
Jonah	**3**: 100-104
Jonathan (son of Abiathar)	**2**: 178, 179, 184, 185, 190
Jonathan (son of Saul)	**2**: 87, 94-96, 119, 121, 122, 126, 128, 130, 156, 164-166
Joseph (husband of Mary)	**4**: 5, 6, 8, 10, 12, 15, 16, 18, 21, 22, 24, 25, 27, 28, 30, 43, 50, 52, 92
Joseph (of Arimathea)	**5**: 74, 146, 147, 168, 169
Joseph (son of Jacob)	**1**: 98-102, 104-108, 110-114; **6**: 37
Joshua (high priest)	**3**: 169
Joshua (leader of Israel)	**1**: 140, 141, 159-162, 190; **2**: 4-6, 10-12, 14-16, 18-20, 22, 25, 29
Josiah	**3**: 16, 124-126, 128, 132
Judah	**1**: 101, 114, 159
Judas Iscariot	**4**: 127, 128; **5**: 90, 91, 134, 142, 143, 150-152
Judas (of Damascus)	**6**: 51
Kish	**2**: 84
Korah	**1**: 165-167
Laban	**1**: 88-90, 92-94, 96
Lazarus	**5**: 60, 68-72, 74, 90, 99; **7**: 137
Leah	**1**: 89, 90
Levi Matthew	**4**: 118-120
Lot	**1**: 61, 64-68
Louis XV	**7**: 89
Lucifer	**1**: 4-6, 24, 32, 138; **7**: 122, 124, 126
Luke	**6**: 88, 154, 160
Luther, Martin	**7**: 36-38, 40-42, 44-46, 48, 54, 59, 82, 147
Lydia	**6**: 86
Maachah	**3**: 19
Machir	**2**: 165
Mahlon	**2**: 42
Malchus	**5**: 143, 144
Manasseh	**3**: 125, 132; **6**: 7
Manoah	**2**: 49, 50
Mark (John)	**6**: 67, 72, 84
Martha	**5**: 60-62, 68, 70-72, 90
Mary (Martha's sister)	**5**: 60-62, 68, 70-71, 89-92
Mary (mother of Jesus)	**4**: 5, 6, 8, 10, 12, 13, 15, 16, 21, 24, 25, 27, 28, 30, 35, 36, 52, 53
Mary (mother of John Mark)	**6**: 67
Mary Magdalene	**5**: 178-180, 182, 189
Matthew	**5**: 86
Melanchthon, Philipp	**7**: 45
Mephibosheth	**2**: 164-166
Merodach-baladan	**3**: 121
Meshach	**3**: 137, 146-150; **6**: 7
Messiah	**3**: 189, 190; **4**: 11, 12, 15, 16, 18, 20-22, 26, 32, 36, 38, 39; 45, 49, 50, 52, 54, 62, 69, 70, 73, 90, 92, 98, 115, 126, 128, 150; **5**: 17, 18, 27, 34-37, 41-42, 44, 64, 65, 68, 72, 74, 75, 89, 91, 99, 101, 121, 151, 155, 175, 183, **6**: 7, 8, 40-42, 70, 95, 99, 105, 118, 168
Micah	**3**: 190
Michael	**6**: 178; **7**: 126
Michal	**2**: 119, 121, 122, 164, 165
Miller, William	**7**: 102-104, 106-108, 110, 112
Miriam	**1**: 117, 118
Mishael	**3**: 133, 137, 140
Mordecai	**3**: 172-175, 178-182
More, Thomas	**7**: 66
Moses	**1**: 116-120, 122-126, 128-130, 133, 134, 136, 137, 140-143, 145-148, 150-152, 155, 159, 161, 162, 165, 166, 169-178, 181, 182; **2**: 10, 49, 82, 151; **3**: 50, 108, 115, 125, 172; **4**: 15, 50, 52, 58; **5**: 27, 28, 30, 35, 41, 183; **6**: 28, 36, 37, 80, 124; **7**: 136, 159
Naaman	**3**: 84-88; **4**: 93

TOPIC	BOOK
Naboth	**3**: 54-56
Nadab (King of Israel)	**3**: 19
Nadab (son of Aaron)	**1**: 150-152
Nahor	**1**: 79
Naomi	**2**: 42-46
Nathan	**2**: 169, 170, 188-190
Nathanael	**4**: 50, 118, 126
Nebuchadnezzar	**3**: 128, 130, 133, 134, 137, 140, 142-144, 146, 148, 149, 152, 154, 156, 157, 159, 168, 185
Necho	**3**: 133
Nehemiah	**6**: 7, 184-186
Nero	**6**: 155, 156, 158, 159, 161, 162, 166; **7**: 12
Nicanor	**6**: 35
Nicodemus	**4**: 62-64; **5**: 74, 146, 147, 169
Noah	**1**: 38-42, 44-48, 50, 60; **3**: 172, 188; **5**: 122; **6**: 4, 5; **7**: 99, 115, 128, 141, 143, 158
Obadiah (Ahab's servant)	**3**: 22, 41
Obed	**2**: 46
Og	**1**: 181, 182; **2**: 15
Omri	**3**: 19, 20
Onesimus	**6**: 150-152, 154
Orpah	**2**: 42, 43
Othniel	**2**: 25
Parmenas	**6**: 35
Paul	**6**: 72, 74-78, 81, 84-86, 88-92, 94-96, 98, 99-102, 104-106, 108-110, 112-116, 118-120, 123-126, 128-130, 132-137, 139-140, 142-145, 147, 148, 150-152, 154-156, 158-163, 186; **7**: 12, 16
Peter	**4**: 49, 50, 96-98, 108-115, 118, 126, 149, 157-159; **5**: 16, 19, 20, 26, 27, 34-36, 94, 95, 119, 132, 133, 138, 139, 143, 144, 150, 179, 184, 187-189; **6**: 12, 14-16, 18-23, 26, 27, 29-32, 46, 54-56, 58-62, 64-68, 71, 81, 164-166, 186; **7**: 12, 95
Petri, Laurentius	**7**: 59, 60
Petri, Olaf	**7**: 59, 60
Philemon	**6**: 150-152
Philip (apostle)	**4**: 49, 50, 87, 118, 126; **5**: 12
Philip (deacon)	**6**: 35, 40-42, 44, 45, 123

TOPIC	BOOK
Pontius Pilate	**4**: 35
Priscilla	**6**: 104
Prochorus	**6**: 35
Rabshakeh	**3**: 116, 117
Rachel	**1**: 88-90, 92, 94, 99
Rebekah	**1**: 78-80, 82, 85, 88
Rehoboam	**3**: 14, 15, 18
Reuben	**1**: 100, 101, 112
Rezon	**3**: 12
Rhoda	**6**: 67
Rich Young Ruler	**5**: 54, 57, 58
Robinson, John	**7**: 73
Ruth	**2**: 42-46
Samaritans	**4**: 66, 67, 69, 72; **5**: 23, 51; **6**: 46
Samson	**2**: 48, 51, 52, 54-58, 60-64
Samuel	**2**: 68, 70-74, 82-84, 86-88, 90-92, 94, 99-102, 136, 137, 151-153; **6**: 6
Sanballat	**3**: 185, 186
Sapphira	**6**: 24-27, 31
Sarah	**1**: 62, 65, 70, 71, 76
Satan	**1**: 6, 24, 26, 27, 32, 46, 55, 178; **2**: 152-154; **3**: 44, 68, 168, 188, 190; **4**: 4, 5, 27, 31, 32, 43-46, 158, 160, 182; **5**: 17-19, 26, 27, 101, 119, 122, 139, 140, 148, 158, 159, 163, 165; **6**: 4, 8, 26, 27, 35, 51, 77, 80, 81, 90, 96, 99, 110, 112, 116, 144, 147, 148, 155, 166, 176, 179, 180, 186-190; **7**: 10, 13, 14, 16, 18, 19, 24, 52, 59, 65, 95, 120, 122-124, 126, 128-130, 132-134, 137, 140-142, 144, 146, 153, 155, 160, 162, 168-172, 174
Saul (king of Israel)	**2**: 83-84, 86-88, 90-92, 94-96, 98-99, 102, 106, 109, 112, 114, 115, 118-122, 124-126, 128-130, 132-134, 142, 143, 150-154, 156, 157, 164-166, 180; **4**: 122; **7**:143
Saul (of Tarsus)	**6**: 36, 38, 40, 44, 48, 50-52, 71, 72
Sceva	**6**: 110
Sennacherib	**3**: 115-118
Sergius Paulus	**6**: 72
Seth	**3**: 188
Shadrach (Hananiah)	**3**:137, 146-150; **6**: 7
Shalmaneser	**3**: 115
Shammah	**2**: 99

TOPIC	BOOK	TOPIC	BOOK
Shaphan	**3**: 125, 126	Tirzah	**3**: 20
Sheba, Queen of	**3**: 8, 10, 11	Titus	**6**: 160; **7**: 7, 8
Shebna	**3**: 116, 117	Titus (General)	**7**: 7, 8
Shem	**1**: 60	Tobiah	**3**: 185
Shemaiah	**3**: 15	Tyndale, William	**7**: 62-66, 147
Shishak	**3**: 18	Tyrannus	**6**: 109
Shunem, Woman of	**3**: 80	Uriah	**2**: 168-170
Sihon	**1**: 180, 181; **2**: 6, 15	Von Tischendorf, Constantin	**7**: 148
Silas	**6**: 84, 89-92, 94, 95, 98-100	Waldenses	**7**: 22-27
Simeon (city of)	**3**: 125	Wesley, Charles	**7**: 80-82, 84-86
Simeon (of the Temple)	**4**: 15, 16, 52	Wesley, John	**7**: 80-82, 84-86
Simeon (son of Jacob)	**1**: 111-113	Widow of Nain	**7**: 137
Simon (A tanner)	**6**: 59, 61	Williams, Roger	**7**: 76, 78
Simon (of Cyrene)	**5**: 160	Wise Men from the East	**4**: 14, 18, 20-22, 52
Simon (Peter)	**4**: 49, 108, 112; **6**: 59-61, 187, 188	Witch of Endor	**2**: 150
Simon (the leper)	**5**: 74, 88, 89, 92	Wolff, Joseph	**7**: 98-100, 103
Simon (the sorcerer)	**6**: 44-46	Wycliffe, John	**7**: 28-30, 32-34, 48, 63, 147
Sisera	**2**: 25, 26	Xerxes (Artaxerxes)	**3**: 169, 172, 184; **7**: 115
Solomon	**2**: 188-190; **3**: 4-6, 8-12, 14-16, 18, 112, 169, 189; **4**: 133; **5**: 23	Zacharias	**4**: 34-36
Squanto	**7**: 74	Zadok (the priest)	**2**: 176-179, 185, 188-190
Standish, Myles	**7**: 74	Zarephath	**3**: 30; **4**: 93
Staupitz	**7**: 40-42	Zebedee	**4**: 96, 126
Stephen	**6**: 34-38, 44, 45, 48, 160; **7**: 10, 11, 103, 115	Zebulun	**2**: 26, 32; **3**: 111
Tabitha	**6**: 56	Zechariah	**3**: 169; **5**: 99
Terah	**1**: 61	Zedekiah	**3**: 129, 130, 133, 134
Teresh	**3**: 173	Zerubbabel	**3**: 169
Thief on the cross	**5**: 164, 165	Ziba	**2**: 165, 166
Thomas	**5**: 70, 186, 187, 189	Zimri	**3**: 19, 20
Timon	**6**: 35	Zwingli, Ulric	**7**: 48-50, 52
Timothy	**6**: 84, 95, 99, 100, 150, 154, 161,